RUSSIAN CULTURE

an Outline

Second Edition,
Revised

George Kalbouss
Associate Professor
The Ohio State University
Department of Slavic Languages
and Literatures

The Ohio State University Libraries
Publications Committee
Columbus, Ohio
1981

Printed in the U.S.A.

LC: 81-82596
ISBN: 0-88215-050-2

Cover design by Will Shively, Nuncio
Cover photography by Sharon Fullerton

CONTENTS

ACKNOWLEDGMENTS

Since the first edition appeared, more than one thousand students have studied Russian Culture at The Ohio State University using this textbook. My thanks are extended to Professors Mateja Matejic, Frank Silbajoris, and Dolores Brzycki for their comments and help in putting this new edition together. Thanks also to Pauline Bean, Sally Rogers, Maureen Donovan, and Neosha Mackey for editing the manuscript. Most of all, my thanks to Sharon Fullerton as general editor, to Eleanor Daniel and Sharon Schwerzel for overseeing the production, and to the members of the OSU Libraries Publications Committee for their help in the publication of this book.

All the excerpts from Russian literary texts were translated by the author.

George Kalbouss
May 1981

PREFACE TO THE FIRST EDITION

The purpose of this book is to outline some of the significant cultural achievements of the Russian people in their literature, music, fine arts and architecture. No pretense is made of presenting an exhaustive survey; the reader is left on his own to pursue those areas which interest him. A bibliography of works currently available in English is appended for this purpose. The works chosen for study in this text are meant to be representative of some specific periods in Russian cultural history while also being relatively well-known and available in books, art reproductions and records.

This outline arose out of a need for background materials in introductory Russian Culture courses currently taught in American universities on the undergraduate level. The target audience is the non-Russian-speaking student who is curious about the Soviet Union and about the Russian people.

It is my belief that the art, music and literature of a people somehow comment more profoundly upon their life than the political and economic structures they set up. Cultures appear to outlive these other manifestations as well as the governments which try to control them. Why this happens I do not fully know; nevertheless, I am fascinated by the subject. Hopefully, this outline will identify some of the dominant themes from Russian Culture.

I certainly would like to thank numerous persons who have supported my efforts in this area over the past twelve years. From Dartmouth College, warmest thanks are extended to Professors Basil Milovsoroff and Richard Sheldon, who served as chairmen while I taught on the staff of the Russian Department. From Ohio State, special thanks go to Professor David Robinson, who helped convince various committees that such a course was worthwhile. Thanks, too, to the many hundreds of students who took this course and contributed numerous times to pleasant ego-inflation. To my wife, Jo Anne, and two daughters, Christina and Katherine, my gratitude for support, endurance, active listening and companionship.

Most of all, I would like to thank Mr. David Norden and Ms. Karen Schmidt, both of the Ohio State University Libraries Publications Committee, who urged that this text should see the light of day. I would like to thank them for overcoming the many difficulties associated with this book but I cannot; with them, the work has been enjoyable and has always seemed extremely easy. Certainly, without them this outline would never have become a reality.

George Kalbouss
Worthington, Ohio
January 1979

THE SOVIET UNION

The Union of Soviet Socialist Republics, or Soviet Union, is the largest nation on earth, territorially measuring 8,649,500 square miles. Its population, as of 1980, is estimated to be over 262 million.

Political Subdivisions

The USSR is divided into various political subdivisions. The major political entities are fifteen Republics. Within the Republics, other administrative units may be found: Autonomous Soviet Socialist Republics (with large national minority concentrations), Krays (sparsely populated areas), Oblasts (either economically or small ethnically identifiable regions), Rayons (districts), and Cities, Villages and Settlements. The more important national issues are decided on the All-Union level in Moscow. The Soviet Republics and their populations are listed in the table on page 4.

Government and the Communist Party

According to its Constitution, the Soviet Union is governed by the Supreme Soviet, which is divided into two houses: the Soviet of Nationalities and the Soviet of the Union. Delegates to the former are determined according to region, and delegates to the latter, according to population (1 per 300,000).

The Union of Soviet

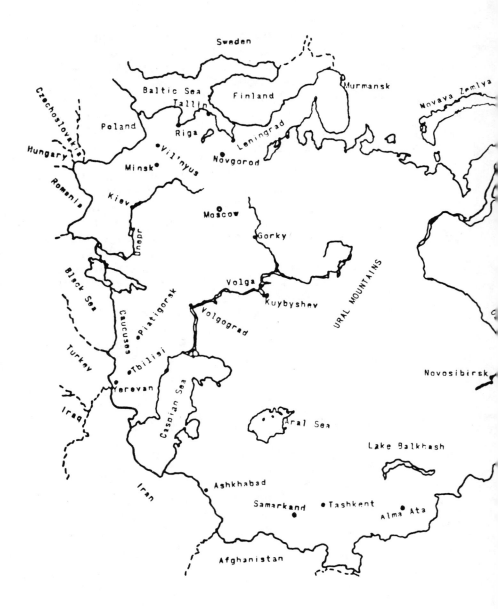

Socialist Republics

The Soviet Socialist Republics are:

REPUBLIC	POPULATION (millions)
EUROPEAN:	
Byelorussian S.S.R.	9.6
* Estonian S.S.R.	1.5
* Latvian S.S.R.	2.5
* Lithuanian S.S.R.	3.4
Moldavian S.S.R.	3.9
Ukrainian S.S.R.	49.8
EUROPEAN AND ASIAN:	
Russian Soviet Federated Socialist Republic	137.5
ASIAN:	
Armenian S.S.R.	3.0
Azerbaijan S.S.R.	6.0
Georgian S.S.R.	5.0
Kazakh S.S.R.	14.7
Kirgiz S.S.R.	3.5
Tadzhik S.S.R.	3.8
Turkmen S.S.R.	2.8
Uzbek S.S.R.	15.4

* The U.S. has never recognized the absorption of the independent states of Latvia, Lithuania and Estonia into the Soviet Union.

The Supreme Soviet meets for only a few days semiannually. The bulk of its work is performed in each of the houses by various committees and commissions and in the Council of Ministers.

The Council of Ministers consists of ministers from various all-Union and Republic minorities as well as agencies and committees. This body is responsible for the operations of the government system; it is the highest executive body of the nation, and its head is the USSR's Prime Minister.

The Presidium of the USSR operates for the Supreme Soviet when it is not in session. This body consists of a President, fifteen vice-presidents, twenty members, and a secretary. The vice-presidents are the presidents of the Soviets of each of the 15 republics.

In actuality, it is the Communist Party of the Soviet Union (CPSU) which determines policy and sets national objectives. Policy, ratified through its All-Union Party Congresses, is established by the Politburo in the Party's Central Committee. It is in the Politburo that both domestic and foreign policy is made. The General Secretary of the CPSU is, in effect, the most powerful individual in the USSR. Party pronouncements are always ratified by the Supreme Soviet and the Council of Ministers.

Only a small percentage of the Soviet population are members of the CPSU: 9% of the adult population. This percentage has become the nation's ruling elite.

Officially, the USSR is still a Socialist state, striving to bring about world Communism. As a Socialist state, it still has classes: laborers, collective farmers, and the intelligentsia. The Communist party is the party of the labor, or working, class.

Cultural Subdivisions

The USSR is a multicultural society. Over 200 languages and dialects are spoken within the nation; each Republic represents one of the more major cultures. In reality, the Russian culture dominates the others; therefore, persons both inside and outside the USSR sometimes refer (erroneously) to the Soviet Union as "Russia." The goal of this textbook is to outline some of the cultural elements of the "Russian" cultural heritage of the USSR.

Life in the USSR

To the outside observer, life is much more controlled in the USSR than in Western Europe or North America. While no longer the police state it was under Stalin, the government discourages open disagreement with its policies and programs. Travel, especially beyond the borders, is strictly monitored for the Soviet citizen, and only a few succeed in receiving permission to visit other nations.

In day-to-day life, the average Soviet leads a much harder existence than his Western counterpart:

1.   Average salary is 200 rubles/month (1 ruble equals approx. $1.50), but both members of the family usually work.

2.   Housing is nominal (if it is state housing)--perhaps 4-12 rubles/month.   Yet, more than 50% of Soviet housing is "non-state," that is, either private or co-operative and fairly expensive.

3.   A Soviet-made Dzhiguli sells for about 7,000 rubles; a Volga for over 20,000. Cars are in great scarcity.

4.   A centralized economy causes repeated shortages in consumer goods.   For the most part, it is not based on supply and demand, but rather on the fulfillment of 5-year plan quotas.   High expenditures on defense have put serious strains on the civilian sectors of the economy.

5.   Medical care is free, but medical services vary from excellent to shoddy.

6.   Everyone is guaranteed a job.

7.   Most Soviets have electricity and television.   Running water exists in the main cities but not in some of the villages.

8.   The main cities, particularly Moscow, Leningrad, Kiev, and the Baltic cities (Riga, Vilnius, Tallinn) are the most attractive to the Russians.   Due to housing shortages, however, they are "closed" unless a person already has a job there and a place to stay.

9.   Despite the hardships, most Russians have available cash; they have learned to "do

without" rather than buy shoddy merchandise that will fall apart. For rare consumer goods, Russians will willingly stand in long lines, risk careers and jail sentences on the black market, and even buy for their friends, assuming that the friends would also want to purchase the same goods. The motto is, "when in doubt, buy."

10. The USSR has the most extensive educational system in the world, ranging from child-care centers and kindergartens to specialized institutes of higher learning. Education is free throughout the USSR. The Soviets claim that all Soviet citizens are guaranteed employment upon the completion of their schooling. Course content is centrally planned and much of it is screened by the CPSU.

11. The bleak picture of the consumer economy does not do justice to the dramatic strides the Soviets have made in improving the average citizen's quality of life. While the pace is slow, the Soviets have greatly increased the number of housing units, the quality of food, and the choices available to the consumer; nevertheless, these strides are still far outdistanced by the non-Communist nations of the West.

SUPREME SOVIET OF THE USSR

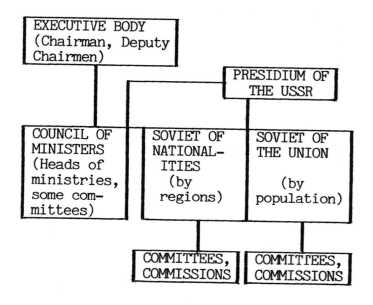

COMMUNIST PARTY OF
THE SOVIET UNION (CPSU)

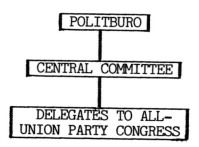

GEOGRAPHY OF THE USSR

The USSR stands in history as the world's largest political entity to be governed from one central location. The geography of the nation poses unique and often serious problems of government and control; these same problems have also created an unusual set of cultural expectations. Three factors control problems created by Soviet geography: size, northern location, and continental climate.

Size

The USSR is the largest nation on earth. It occupies 8,649,500 square miles. For comparison, the U.S. occupies 3,675,633 square miles; Canada, 3,851,809. The continent of Europe occupies 3,835,000 square miles; South America, 6,870,000 square miles. These statistics acquire meaning when compared to some more familiar data:

1. The entire earth has 57,230,000 square miles of land. The USSR occupies 15% of the world's surface. If the entire world's population was placed in the USSR, it would have the population density of Connecticut.

2. Size implies great distance: the USSR covers eleven time zones. Moscow to Vladivostok is 5,778 miles; Brest to Moscow is an additional 683, totalling 6461 miles from the Polish border to Vladivostok. Even from north to south, the distances are close to coast-to-coast distances in the United States:

Murmansk to Leningrad	700 miles
Leningrad to Moscow	356 miles
Moscow to Erevan	1791 miles
	2847 miles

(Compare: New York
to Los Angeles   2915 miles)

3. Size also implies "time" problems. Transportation of materials and people over great distances requires time. In Siberia, a good railroad is imperative since the rivers do not flow the right way for commerce. The Trans-Siberian Express leaves daily from Moscow to Vladivostok; it departs Moscow at 10:05 a.m. on the first day, arrives in Novosibirsk at 10:31 a.m. on the third day, in Irkutsk at 6:47 p.m. on the fourth day, and in Vladivostok at 1:40 p.m. on the eighth day of travel.

Northern Location

The USSR is one of the northernmost nations on earth, together with Canada, the U.S. (Alaska), Greenland, Norway, and Finland.

1. The "southern" resort area of the Black Sea is still on the level of Fargo, North Dakota. Moscow is located on the level of Hudson Bay, and Leningrad is on the level of Anchorage, Alaska.

2. The extreme northern location also presents the problem of permafrost--of soil not having thawed out since glaciation. This situation renders road-building almost impossible and creates serious problems such

as trees cracking when they are chopped down and buildings sinking into the mud created by their own heat.

3. Since the major Siberian rivers flow northward, they flood in the spring as the thawed water of the south reaches the iced-up parts of the rivers. The northern flow of the rivers has rendered them of little use in the transportation of raw materials from Siberia to the western industrial cities. With few frost-free days, only 11% of the USSR is arable. The Ukraine, the bread-basket of the USSR, averages only 150-180 frost-free days per year, a figure close to the period needed to grow wheat (115 frost-free days for winter wheat and 136 for summer).

4. Many of the USSR's agricultural problems are a result of its northern location rather than poor management. The virgin lands campaign of Khrushchev (an attempt to expand outwardly the growing of wheat and corn rather than to get more yield per acre) helped bring about his demise. Methods are now changing, and Soviets are looking to the U.S. for agricultural expertise. With an average frost-free period close to that of the time needed to grow wheat, one can depend upon periodic crop failures in the USSR.

5. The USSR's northern location also influences the amount of daylight available in a region during various seasons. In the far north, daylight is plentiful in the summer, creating the pleasant "white nights"; on the other hand, darkness reigns in winter, with little or no daylight available in cities like Leningrad and Murmansk.

Continental Climate

The large land mass of the USSR, relatively far away from the moderating influences of the oceans, gives the nation a continental climate. The condition creates:

1. Greater extremes in temperature during each day and between seasons.

2. Some extreme cold spots in the USSR. The coldest place in the world (except for Antarctica) is Verkhoyansk in Siberia. Its mean temperature in January is -40° F. The record low temperature, -89° F, was recorded in Oymyakon, in Siberia. In European Russia, the coldest temperature was recorded in Ust-Shchugor, -67° F.

3. Little access to the prevailing west-to-east winds emanating from the Atlantic Ocean. Even the fertile Ukraine receives winds which have already passed over Western Europe.

RUSSIAN, THE SLAVIC LANGUAGES, AND THE MISSION OF CYRIL AND METHODIUS

Russian and the Slavic Languages

Russian is one of many languages of the Indo-European language chain and is thus distantly related to English, German, and French. It is a member of the Slavic language family, as the diagram shows:

West Slavic

Polish (Poland)
Czech (Czechoslovakia)
Slovak (Czechoslovakia)
Upper Sorbian (E. Germany)
Lower Sorbian (E. Germany)

South Slavic

Slovenian (Yugoslavia)
** Serbo-Croatian (Yugoslavia)
 * Macedonian (Yugoslavia)
 * Bulgarian (Bulgaria)
 * Old Church Slavonic

East Slavic

 * Byelorussian (USSR)
 * Ukrainian (USSR)
 * RUSSIAN (USSR)

Due to historically religious differences, the Slavic languages use two alphabets. Those without an asterisk use the Latin alphabet (as 'does English) and have a Roman Catholic background. Those with an asterisk (*) use the Cyrillic alphabet, which was especially created for the Slavic languages; these languages have an Eastern Orthodox religious heritage. Serbo-Croatian (marked with **) has a unique heritage: the Serbs have an Eastern Orthodox heritage and therefore use Cyrillic, while the Croats have a Roman Catholic heritage and use Latin letters. Thus this one language has two alphabets.

The Mission of Cyril and Methodius

The alphabet used by the Russians was, for the most part, a creation of two brothers: Constantine, later sainted as Cyril (826-69), and Methodius (815-85). The creation of an alphabet for the Slavs coincided with that time in history when the various Slavic tongues were emerging as separate languages. Thus the work of Cyril and Methodius sheds a great deal of light on the process of the evolution of the Slavic language family.

The mission of Cyril and Methodius to the Slavs was a result of a request by Prince Rastislav of Great Moravia (reigned 846-69) to Michael III, Emperor of Byzantium, to obtain an alphabet for his people as well as a Christian liturgy. Rastislav was also anxious to retard the expansion of two of his neighbors--Bulgaria to the east and the Frankish states to the west--and thus wanted an alliance with Byzantium.

GLAGOLITIC/ CYRILLIC/ MODERN RUSSIAN ALPHABETS

Glagolitic	Cyrillic	Mod. Russian	Closest English equiv.	
ⰀⰊⰅⱅ	ⰀⰂ Ⰰ	А а	A	"arch"
ⰂⰡⰃ	Б	Б б	B	"boat"
Ⰲ	В	В в	V	"very"
ⰋⰆ	Г	Г г	G	"goat"
Ⰾ	Д	Д д	D	"deal"
	Ⰵ	Е е	Yeh	"yes"
Ⰶ	Ж	Ж ж	Zh	"azure"
Ⰸ	ЗⰅ	З з	Z	"zoom"
Ⱃⱁ ⱝ	Ⰻ		I	"feel"
Ⰹ	И	И и	I	"feel"
Ⰼ		Я я	Jot	"yellow"
Ⰽ	К	К к	K	"kite"
Ⰾ	Ⰾ	Л л	L	"love"
Ⰿ	М	М м	M	"money"
Ⱀ	Н	Н н	N	"none"
Ⱁ	Ⱁ	О о	O	"oar"
Ⱂ	п	П п	P	"post"
Ⱃ	Р	Р р	R	"row"
Ⱄ	С	С с	S	"sock"
Ⱅ	Т	Т т	T	"toss"

Glagolitic	Cyrillic	Mod. Russian	Closest English Equiv.
(glag.)	оу, ȣ	у у	Oo "r<u>oo</u>m"
(glag.)	ф	Ф ф	F "<u>f</u>ind"
(glag.)	ѳ		Theta "<u>th</u>ing"
(glag.)	х	Х х	Kh "ba<u>ck h</u>ome"
(glag.)	ѡ		O "<u>oa</u>r"
(glag.)	ψ		Sht
(glag.)	ц	Ц ц	Ts "<u>ts</u>etse"
(glag.)	ч	Ч ч	Ch "<u>ch</u>arm"
(glag.)	ш	Ш ш	Sh "<u>sh</u>ark"
	щ	Щ щ	Shch "fi<u>sh ch</u>illed"
(glag.)	ь	ь	Soft sign
(glag.)	ы	ы	Y "Chi<u>c</u>ago"
(glag.)	ъ	ъ	Hard sign
(glag.)	ѣ	ѣ	Jat. "v<u>e</u>ry" (replaced by "e")
(glag.)	є	э э	Eh "<u>e</u>very"
(glag.)	ю	ю ю	Yu "<u>you</u>"
	ꙗ	я я	Ya "<u>ya</u>k"
(glag.)	ѧ		nasal "e"
(glag.)	ѫ		nasal "o"

(N.B. Not all letters of the glagolitic and
older Cyrillic are reproduced)

The mission to Great Moravia was led by two brothers from Thessalonica who were Greeks by birth but of Slavic parentage. Their language was a South Slavic dialect. Since at that time in history all Slavs could probably understand each other, it was relatively simple to adopt their dialect to that of the Great Moravians. Cyril and Methodius created a new symbol-system in which one symbol equalled one sound.

To this day, Cyril and Methodius's system provides the basis for the alphabets of all the Slavs of the Eastern Orthodox heritage. The language of the first texts is called Old Church Slavonic. While it has died as a spoken language, it still provides the foundations for the liturgical languages of the Slavic Eastern Orthodox churches. Cyril and Methodius's original symbol system is called Glagolitic. A simplification of this system-- but not a departure from its general principles--made by the brothers' followers in Bulgaria is called Cyrillic in honor of Cyril. The table on pages 16 and 17 shows the evolution of the alphabet from the original Glagolitic to today's Russian.

RUSSIAN ORTHODOXY

The Russian Orthodox Church represents the Russian branch of the Eastern Orthodox faith. The term "Orthodox" means "right-praising" or "right-believing." Orthodox believers trace the origins of their religion to the early Christian church. Until 1917, the Russian Orthodox Church was the official church of the Russian state; in the USSR the church is tolerated, but participation in its rituals is discouraged.

The Traditions of Eastern Orthodox Christianity

1. The Orthodox Church founds its beliefs on ancient Christian traditions. These traditions are anchored in various documents, books, laws, rituals, and sacred objects.

2. The Bible (using the apocryphal books: Esdras 2, 3; Tobit, Judith, etc.) forms the historical background for understanding God's work in man's world. The Orthodox Church is a scriptural church, but the Bible functions within the church and not over it. Biblical interpretation, therefore, is done by the Church through the inspiration of God.

3. The Eastern Orthodox Church accepts all creeds ratified before the Schism of the 11th century. Orthodoxy emphasizes the unity of the Trinity, as stated in the Nicene Creed. In matters of faith, the Orthodox Church acknowledges the authority and pronouncements of the Seven Ecumenical Councils (325-787). Orthodox believers hope

that, some day, an Eighth Ecumenical Council will take place which will unite eastern and western churches.

4. The Church celebrates the lives of various saints and fathers of the Church. Of these, the greatest Church hierarchs are: Gregory of Nazianus, Basil the Great and St. John Chrysostom.

5. The Orthodox Church is a liturgical church. The Church's ritual lives within the Church traditions and symbolizes man's attempts to revere God. The liturgy likewise conveys some of God's mysteries. The Bible, divided into lessons, is read in the liturgy.

6. The Orthodox Church has developed numerous rules and laws; many regulations are well-defined and strict. The Church has both dogma and canon law.

7. Icons are works of religious art which establish communion between God and man. The term icon means "image" The art of the icon forces man to focus his worship on its meaning and to capture a glimpse of what is eternal in the universe. Initially, man is the "icon" of God (made in God's own image). Icons are "blessed" in special services, and are considered objects of veneration.

The Nature of God and Man

1. In the Orthodox faith, God is absolutely transcendent and the ruler of the entire universe. God's essence cannot be explained by logic; He simply exists.

2. God and man are in a relationship of estrangement, but one which has hope for reconciliation. God is not cut off from His world; He works and lives within it through the Church.

3. God is trinitarian and contains within Him three persons (Father, Son, and Holy Spirit). Each of the three persons contains the other two as well. This relationship is essentially a mystery.

4. Through Jesus, God has become incarnate. He has loved the world so much that he became one of his own creatures.

5. God's love for man is expressed in the freedom that He has given him. Man has free will, but he must choose God's way as it is shown him by the Church.

6. Jesus' life is symbolic of the perfect life. His teachings and miracles provide the basis for the Christian faith. In addition, several "mysteries" are associated with Jesus: the incarnation, the transfiguration and the resurrection.

7. In icons, God is depicted both as the Victim and the Victor. One does not exist without the other. Jesus' suffering on the cross was but a temporal step leading to His triumph over death.

8. The Church continues the work of Jesus' disciples through Apostolic Succession. All Orthodox bishops, therefore, are descended in spirit from St. Peter.

9. It is possible for all persons to become saints since all participate in God's

divine nature. Sainthood results from a pious life, but one that is not so difficult that no one can accomplish it. Sainthood thus is:

    a. Democratic: available to everyone.

    b. Realistic: even when one is a saint, one is still aware of sin.

    c. Methodical: ordinary but disciplined men and women can achieve sainthood following the regulations of the church.

    d. Communal: sainthood is achieved by loving one's neighbor.

    e. Practical: sainthood attains positive results; it improves the lot of man.

The Church

1. Orthodox dogma states that the Church is united and infallible and only within the Orthodox church can one find salvation. The Church, like the Trinity, is unified.

2. The Church is hierarchical in structure, having both rank and titles. In the Orthodox church they are:

Rank	Title
Bishop	Bishop
	Archbishop
	Metropolitan
	Patriarch
Priest	Priest
	Archpriest
Deacon	Deacon
	Archdeacon

Only bishops· may ordain. Parish priests may marry before ordination, but monks may not marry.

The Orthodox Worship Service

1. The Orthodox worship service is highly structured, emphasizing aesthetic beauty. Much of the service consists of chanting and responses.

2. The liturgy, at the center of the service, is held "in the language of the people." In some cases, however, the church language is slightly more archaic than the spoken secular tongue, since it has not changed as much over the centuries. In the Russian Church, the language is called "Russian Church Slavonic," since it traces its roots to the Church Slavonic tradition of Cyril and Methodius.

3. The liturgy is performed communally. The worshippers stand in an open area facing the icon-screen (iconostasis) behind which is the altar. The icon-screen has three doors; the middle door is the Royal Door and may be entered only by an ordained clergyman. The altar always faces east.

4. Most Orthodox churches are square in their plan, surmounted by a dome.

5. The music of the Orthodox church is sung a capella, that is, without any musical accompaniment. The only musical sounds worthy of praising God come from the human voice and the churchbell.

6. Worshippers may use the sign of the cross many times. Sometimes the sign is prescribed by the liturgy; at other times worshippers cross themselves when they are moved to do so.

7. The Orthodox church observes seven sacraments:

    a. Baptism
    b. Chrismation
    c. Eucharist (Orthodox believers contend that transubstantiation takes place during the Eucharist celebration)
    d. Confession
    e. Marriage
    f. Ordination
    g. Anointing of the sick

8. The Orthodox church still observes the old Julian calendar; it does not recognize the Gregorian calendar reform of 1582. As a result, the Orthodox church calendar is currently 13 days behind the Gregorian calendar. Russian Christmas, for example is celebrated (according to the new calendar) on January 7th. The Bolshevik "October Revolution" actually took place on November 7th.

KIEVAN RUS' AND
THE BYZANTINE TRADITION

The city of Kiev is claimed by both the Russian and Ukrainian cultures as their cultural ancestor. Legends relate that the eastern Slavs began to settle in the area of Kiev in the 7th and 8th centuries. One legend mentions that three brothers settled the region: Kii, Sheck, and Khoriv. Possibly, these names originally related to three early Slav settlements.

Early History of Kiev

The early history of Kiev is recorded in the Chronicles, which were maintained by monks, who recorded the legends and day-to-day histories of the city-state. Scholars have compiled a document called The Primary Chronicle, which relates the important events of this period, including:

1. 9th century: Kiev is invaded by the Scandinavian Vikings, the so-called "Varangians." Rurik (Roerich) of Jutland, who plunders France, Britain, and Germany, also journeys on a route between the Baltic Sea and Byzantium, (the "route from the Varyags to Byzantium,") following the river systems through Novgorod and Kiev.

2. 862: Rurik is "invited" to be prince over the Kievans. The term "Rus'" is introduced with his ascendancy to the throne. Rus' is also a term associated with the Swedes. Rurik takes power and makes Novgorod the seat of his rule.

3. 904-7: Oleg, Rurik's successor, wages war against Constantinople. Legends relate that he "kissed the cross," that is, converted to Christianity.

4. 956-72: Reign of Prince Svyatoslav who battles the Jewish Khazars in the east. His mother, Olga, was a Christian.

5. 988-89: The adoption of Christianity. Prince Vladimir adopts Byzantine Christianity as part of an alliance with the Byzantine emperor Basil II (976-1025). In order to marry Basil's sister Anne, Vladimir is baptized in 988-89. The Chronicle legend of Kiev's Christianization relates that Vladimir sent emissaries to choose among the various religions: the Muslims (Bulgars), Jews (Khazars), Western Christians (Germans), and Eastern Christians (Byzantines). The emissaries were filled with awe and wonder as they entered the Church of Hagia Sophia in Constantinople: "They did not know where they were, on heaven or on earth," and they recommended that Byzantine Christianity be adopted by the Kievan prince.

6. 1019-54: The rule of Yaroslav the Wise. During Yaroslav's rule the Cathedral of St. Sophia in Kiev was begun (1037). Yaroslav solidified Kievan power and projected it toward neighboring territories. During his reign the code of law, the Russkaya Pravda (Russian Justice), was begun.

7. 1113-1125: The rule of Vladimir Monomakh. Monomakh's reign was the last which achieved unity for Kiev. After his short reign, the various Kievan princes continued to feud with each other, thus

permitting outside invaders to divide and conquer them. Monomakh's <u>Testament</u> to his children provides a unique insight into the practical mind of this Kievan leader.

8. 1240: Kiev falls to the army of Batu Khan.

The Byzantine Tradition

The Byzantine tradition inherited by the Kievans was a sophisticated and complex one, developed over centuries from early Christianity and Platonism. Few Kievans understood this tradition; nevertheless, many patterns of Byzantine culture were adopted in the new Christian state.

1. The architectural pattern for most Russian churches is based on the floorplan of Hagia Sophia in Constantinople: a square surmounted by a dome. This plan may be seen in the churches of St. Sophia in both Kiev and Novgorod.

2. The Kievo-Pecherskaya Lavra, or "Crypt Monastery," was one of the earliest religious settlements in Kiev, built in the side of a hill overlooking the Dniepr River. It was in this monastery that many entries into the <u>Chronicles</u> were written. Today it is a museum.

3. The Kievan church of St. Sophia both followed Byzantine traditional artistic patterns and developed some of its own. Frescoes on the walls depict not only sacred subjects but also secular ones, showing mummers entertaining the Kievan court.

4. Kievan religious painting was adopted from Byzantine traditions. The religious paintings are called icons, meaning "images." Kievan icons, for the most part, adhere strictly to Byzantine rules. Novgorod icons are characterized by strong white highlighting of figures as well as a dominant red color. Few icons of these early times have survived, but several are very famous: Our Lady of Vladimir (The Mother-of-God of Tenderness, late 11th to early 12th century) and The Angel of the Golden Hair (12th century). Each medieval Russian city developed its own icon style.

5. Kievan literature was strongly Byzantine in flavor; much of it consisted of Byzantine translations. The oldest original Kievan literature is based mostly on historical and religious themes.

The Song of Igor's Campaign

An unusual work from this period is The Song of Igor's Campaign, a written epic describing the defeat of the troops of Prince Igor of Novgorod-Seversk whose expedition fell to the Polovtsy in 1185-87. This work has been lauded by many as a masterpiece of medieval epic writing.

Written using the brilliant imagery of the oral epic which is then transformed into a sophisticated, complex poetic creation, the Igor tale recounts one of the incidents which hastened the downfall of Kiev. The "hero" of this epic, Prince Igor, disregards his brothers' warnings about attacking the invading Polovtsy without any help from them and is defeated in his attempt. His impetuous act of pride contributed to the demoralization of the Kievan forces by weakening them considerably and helped destroy the aspirations of the more mature leaders of Kiev to defend themselves against the outsiders. This work of an anonymous poet, discovered at the end of the 18th century, has been lauded as one of the great poetic creations of Russian culture. In the 19th century, it provided the inspiration for Aleksandr Borodin's opera <u>Prince Igor</u>.

MOSCOW AND THE FEUDAL PERIOD

The Tatar Yoke

Due to internal disagreements and persistent attacks from the outside, the state of Kiev began to disintegrate in the 12th century. The lack of a viable military center made all the Russian cities of that time prey to various non-Russian tribes; and in 1223, the Russians were defeated at the river Kalka by the Mongols led by Genghis Khan. From that time until the battle of Kulikovo in 1380, most of the Russian lands were under the domination of the so-called "Tatar yoke." Only the free city of Novgorod, with its strong economic ties to Western Europe through the Hanseatic League, escaped conquest conquered by the Mongols.

Life of a conquered people is considerably different from that of a free one. The Russians had to contend with working for alien lords, with paying tribute, and with cruel, repressive political control. The two hundred years of alien rule may have created what some observers see as a "passive" Russian response to governmental indignities, that is, a tradition of enduring various repressions rather than confronting them openly, of appearing to "go along" while not strongly agreeing or disagreeing with some policy.

The Rise of Monasticism

The Mongol period and the 14th to 15th centuries saw a dramatic rise in monastic movements, many of which searched for the inner peace that the violent outside world did not provide. One hundred and eighty monasteries were built in the 14th and 15th centuries, and another 300 in the 15th and 16th centuries.

It was probably also during this time that the great oral epics, or byliny, began to be sung, recalling the better times of the Russian people in a semimythological Kievan "Camelot" ruled by Prince Vladimir and defended by various brave knights, or bogatyrs, notably, Ilya Murometz, Dobrinya Nikitich, and Alyosha Popovich. From that time on, these heroes became the Russian oral tradition's heroes of the people, defenders of the faith, and symbols of an irrepressible Russian spirit.

The Rise of Moscow

It was during the Mongol period that the city-state of Moscow began to grow. In the 12th century, Moscow was yet another city-state, not much different from other similar cities: Vladimir, Suzdal and Yaroslavl. Yet, the Moscow Princes managed to mollify the Mongol lords and consolidate their power at the same time, thus acquiring the legacy of Kiev.

1. In 1261, Daniel, the son of Alexander Nevsky, moved to Moscow. By doing so, he brought the name of the Rurik dynasty to Moscow. Between 1283 and 1304, he formed the Moscow state.

2. In 1326, the Metropolitan of the Russian Orthodox church moved his seat to

Moscow, giving Moscow not only the secular legacy of the Rurik house, but also the sacred legacy of the Christian church.

3. By 1380, the Moscow Princes managed to assemble enough strength to defeat the Mongols at the field of Kulikovo. The Moscow Prince who led the battle, Dmitry of the Don (Dmitry Donskoi), became a real (rather than fictitious) symbol of Russian bravery and fortitude. His name has been frequently invoked by later Russian rulers to arouse patriotic fervor.

The Building of the Kremlin

With the demise of the Mongols, the city of Moscow began to grow even more swiftly. Moscow's Kremlin, one of many such walled cities remaining from Russia's medieval period, has since become the world's symbol for Soviet might.

1. Little is known of the early Moscow Kremlin (14th to 15th centuries). At that time, the Kremlin was made of white stone; the walls perhaps resembled those of the current Troitsko-Sergeyevskaya Lavra at Zagorsk, at the outskirts of Moscow. The current Kremlin's construction, begun in 1470, was conducted mainly by Italians: Marko Ruffo, Peter Solari, Anton and Aleviz Fryazin, and Aristotle Fioravanti.

2. The wall around the Kremlin, with its evenly spaced towers, is a work of art in itself. Even the bricks were prescribed to be of uniform size: 30 x 14 x 7 cm.; 8 kg. Towers were placed at every bend in the

wall, and the height of the wall was kept at a uniform level in most places, even if it meant filling in low areas and channeling streams inside the Kremlin walls (5-19 m. high, 3.5-6.5 m. thick).

3. The Kremlin's main entry is the Spassky Tower. Its clock, added in 1625 and replaced several times, tells the "official time" for the entire Soviet Union. Five of the towers have entrances.

4. One of the early structural masterpieces is the belltower of Ivan the Great (1505-8), which is the highest structure in the Kremlin. It is 81 meters high, dominating the Kremlin skyline.

5. The Uspensky (Assumption) Cathedral (1475-79), the most massive of the churches in the Kremlin, houses many artistic treasures, including icons by Andrei Rublev. Its interior is made up of evenly spaced columns covered with iconic representations. The building suffered through slight earth tremors and was reinforced with iron in 1626.

6. The Blagoveshchensky (Annunciation) Cathedral (1484-89) was built for the tsar's family's private worship. Its towers were added later, thus creating a contrast in styles.

7. The Rispolozhenskaya (Deposition) Church was first built in 1484 to celebrate Moscow's triumph over the Khan Mazovshe. In 1517 it was torn down and a new structure was erected in its place. This second church is considered by many to be one of the finest examples of 16th century Russian church architecture.

8. The Archangel Michael Cathedral (1505-9) was built by Italians (Aleviz the younger), as is shown by the Venetian shell ornaments under the roofs. Due to its location near other structures, it is the darkest of all the Kremlin churches.

9. The "Terem" Palace was constructed in 1635-36 and is characterized by its numerous facades. Since then, additional buildings have been added to the Kremlin. The most recent is the Soviet Palace of Congresses, completed in 1961.

10. The Moscow period also witnessed the work of Russia's greatest icon painter, Andrei Rublev (c. 1360-1430), whose works have been compared favorably to the greatest Italian masters'. His subdued colors, contrasted with a bright light blue and yellow-orange, and the peaceful countenances of his subjects mark his unique style. His most famous icon is The Old Testament Trinity (1420), a symbolic representation of the Eucharist which shows three angels seated about a Eucharistic table.

Moscow As Capital of Russia

As Moscow grew, it centralized its power and became a symbol of Russian autocracy to the rest of the world. Many of the images of Russian cruelty have been centered around Ivan "the Terrible" (more literally, in Russian, "the awesome") (1530-84), who helped solidify the rule of Moscow over her surroundings. Ilya Repin's painting Ivan the Terrible and his son Ivan, 16 November 1581 (1885) depicts the tsar's reputed darkest deed, the murder of his eldest son. Insights into Ivan's mind may be found in the Ivan-Kurbsky Correspondence, a collection of letters between the tsar and a nobleman who had escaped to Lithuania.

Ivan's architects, Posnik and Barma, built the elaborate Cathedral of Basil the blessed (1554-60) on Red Square. Named after a simpleton who made prophecies to the tsar, the church combines various architectural styles, notably those of "tent" and "onion" domed churches. It is the most frequently depicted church of the USSR. The domes were not immediately painted; the coloring was done under Catherine the Great.

Following Ivan's death, Moscow underwent a "Time of Troubles" (1598-1613), in which the new nation was besieged by internal and external enemies. His son-in-law, Boris Godunov (1551-1605), remained on the throne for a brief time (1598-1605) but died during the first of several Polish invasions. Finally, the nation stabilized under the rule of the Romanovs, who remained in power until the revolutions of 1917. The Time of Troubles is depicted in Pushkin's play (and Mussorgsky's opera) Boris Godunov.

The Schism

Orthodox Church reforms in the late 17th century, which were intended to return the Russian church to the practices of the early Christian church as practiced on Mt. Athos, created a "Great Schism" and caused a body of Christian believers to break away to establish their own faith. Calling themselves "Old Believers," they spurned the reforms instituted by Patriarch Nikon as works of the Antichrist. A valuable insight into the world of Old Believers may be found in the autobiographical Life of the Archpriest Avvakum (1620-82), a vivid account of an ardent Old Believer's battle with the forces of the established Orthodox Church. Surikov's painting Boyarinya Morozova (1887) captures the figure of a wealthy Old Believer being taken away for execution while defiantly giving the sign of an Old Believer two-fingered (rather than "reformed" Orthodox three-fingered) blessing.

The Rise of Poetry and Drama

Increased contacts with the west through Poland and the Ukraine brought new influences in the literary arts and the theater. Russian poetry, using Polish poetic structures, was written by Simeon Polotsky (1629-80), who had been educated at the western-influenced Kiev Academy (founded 1624). The first Russian play, The Play of Artaxerxes by the Lutheran Pastor Johann Gregory, was staged on October 17, 1672, in a private showing to Tsar Alexei Mikhailovich.

Moscow Today

Moscow continued to grow during the 18th and 19th centuries, even though the nation's energies were going to the construction of St. Petersburg, the new capital. Since much of Moscow was wooden before the great fire of 1812, we may only suppose what it looked like. Moscow remained the cultural center of Russia into the 1830s and '40s, with many of the older aristocratic families remaining in the old capital. After 1918, it became the capital once again.

Today Moscow sprawls for hundreds of square miles, connected by a famous subway system--one of the world's most efficient.

Notable sites, besides the Kremlin, include:

1. The Novodevichy monastery, which contains the graves of many notable Russian authors and musicians. Its 17th-century iconastasis is one of the city's most elaborately ornamented ones.

2. The Bolshoi theater (19th century), one of the many buildings, particularly in the downtown area, built in a neo-classical style in imitation of St. Petersburg buildings.

3. Kolomenskoe with the Church of the Ascension, one of the finest examples of Russian tent-domed architecture.

4. The University of Moscow, an imposing structure of the "wedding-cake" architecture popular under Stalin, dominating the high banks of the Moscow River in the area of the Lenin Hills.

5. The Moscow outdoor pool, one of the world's largest, operating all winter long.

6. Hotel Rossia, next to Red Square, one of the world's largest hotels.

7. The downtown area on Novy Arbat, as modern as any European downtown.

8. The Moscow Metro, an efficient subway system with elaborate stations.

9. Monuments, such as <u>Worker and Collective Farmer</u> by Mukrina and the Space Monument at the Exposition of Domestic Achievements.

The Troitsko-Sergeevskaya Lavra Monastery near Moscow at Zagorsk.

Posnik and Barma. Cathedral of Basil the Blessed. Red Square. 1554-60.

Church of the Ascension. Kolomenskoe. Moscow, 1530–32.

Aristotle Fioravanti. The Assumption (Uspensky) Cathedral. Moscow, Kremlin.

NEOCLASSICISM AND THE
BUILDING OF ST. PETERSBURG

Russia made her great "leap forward" and became a modern European state in the 18th century, mainly due to the efforts of Peter the Great and Catherine the Great. It was during this time that Europe was in her "neoclassical" period, emphasizing interest in the "classical" heritage of Greece and Rome.

Peter the Great

The foundations for a modern Russian state were laid by Peter the Great (1672-1725), who felt that Russia had no choice but to accept Western ways. Peter's most enduring testament to his reforms is his city, St. Petersburg (now Leningrad), constructed on the Gulf of Finland as his "window on the West." Construction began in 1703; one hundred years later, St. Petersburg was one of Europe's most beautiful cities.

As a youth, Peter endured numerous palace intrigues and power struggles. Travelling to the West as a young man, he learned various manual trades and was impressed by the Protestant work ethic. When he received the total power of his office, he quickly took steps to rid Russia of her "old" ways and to build in their stead a nation based on Western European practices. To some, he became the savior of Russia; to others, he was the Antichrist. His edicts (ukazy) were treated as military orders; not to shave off one's beard meant death on the chopping block. To acquire badly needed financial credits, Peter melted gold from icons and church roofs. He instituted a civil service system which promoted on merit rather than on family ties.

Peter's reforms are celebrated in Falconet's statue, Monument to Peter I (1765-82), in which Peter, mounted on his horse, is stamping out the serpent of ignorance. A fascinating figure, Peter has been the subject of numerous literary works, as has been his city. The Falconet statue forms the central image in Pushkin's tale-in-verse, The Bronze Horseman (1835); two novels about Peter are: D. Merezhkovsky's Peter and Alexis (1905) and A. N. Tolstoy's Peter the First (1929-45).

Neoclassicism

Throughout Europe, neoclassicism was a movement which sought to simplify and purify the excesses of the Baroque tradition. Its models, the Greek and Roman classics, provided the simple forms for literature and art based on reason rather than on emotions. To the neoclassical theorist, the ordered and beautiful city, rather than the chaotic and disordered countryside, provided the environment for contemplating the eternal truths of the universe. Nature was good only when cultivated; the "park" was far more preferable than the "forest."

Russian Painting

Until the 18th century, Russian art was essentially the art of the icon. In the 18th century, and for the first time in history, Russian art became secular. Most 18th-century Russian paintings are portraits: I. Nikitin's portrait of Peter I (early 18th century), D. Levitsky's E. Khovanskaya and E. Khrushcheva (1773) and A. Lansky (1782). Following European practices, Russian neoclassical paintings "idealize" their subjects, that is, present them without blemishes, as they "should be."

Russian Literature

1. Eighteenth-century Russian literature also began by drawing its images from the secular traditions of Western Europe; indeed, many themes of the earlier 18th—century literature are adopted from the French. Antioch Kantemir (1708-44), one of Russia's first neoclassicists, learned his craft in the West, where he served in various diplomatic posts. His work, while not of a very high quality, nevertheless searches to find something Russian in popular French themes. Patterned after French imitations of Roman satires, his own works poke fun at the boorishness of the Russian landed gentry, who believe that only the outer trappings of genteel living are important. In "Satire I. To His Own Wit," he writes of two such Russians, Luke and Medor:

> Burping thrice, rosy-cheeked
>   Luke says again,
> Science wrecks the great friend
>   ships of men . . .
> Medor cries that too much just
>   transpires
> On letters, print, but as for

his desires
He cannot get his curly locks to
  twist.
Seneca's not for wigs; Medor
  wants powd'ry mist.

In this work, we find an attempt to poke fun at the hypocrisies of the Russian gentry; in the 19th century this tradition will be greatly expanded by Gogol, Saltykov-Shchedrin and Chekhov.

2. Vasily Tredyakovsky (1703-69), son of an Astrakhan priest, served Catherine the Great as court poet and Secretary of the Academy of Sciences. In imitation of Polish and French poetry, he wrote his earlier poems in "syllabic verse," where the number of syllables remains constant in each line of verse.   Later, he changed his ideas and wrote in "syllabo-tonic verse," where the verse line is made from both constant numbers of syllables and stress patterns, a form more natural to the Russian language.

3. Mikhail Lomonosov (1711-65), inventor, theoretician, poet, and linguist, was a true child of the enlightenment and may be regarded as a "Benjamin Franklin" of Russian culture--even to an experiment with a kite and lightning (although his assistant was electrocuted in the experiment). His essay on the "levels of style" in Russian poetry, prose, and drama established a standard which influenced most 19th-century Russian writing. His interest in science inspired some poetry on scientific themes: "Meditations on the Evening concerning God's Majesty under the Circumstances of the Northern Lights" posits Lomonosov's metaphysical reflections on

science and discusses the bipolar aspects of electrical energy as released by lightning and (erroneously, as it turned out) the phenomenon of the Aurora Borealis. His "Letter on the Usefulness of Glass" attempts to find the poetic in a mundane technological subject.

4. Gavrila Derzhavin (1743-1816) stands as Russia's greatest poet of the 18th century. Writing in a style with vivid images devoid of cliches, Derzhavin probes the eternal questions of life and death and conveys an awareness of the smallness of man in the universe. In his "Ode on the Death of Prince Meshchersky," he does not see God giving man eternal life:

Death, a shudder, life and
    fright,
We're--pride and poverty
    together.
Today it's God, tomorrow night,
Today it's hope for fairer
    weather.
But then, man, where have you
    gone?
The clocks have barely struck
    the hour,
And you have plunged to Chaos
    dour,
And, as a dream, your life is
    done.

Derzhavin's conclusion is existential; one should live for the day rather than for a hereafter:

Life's but a gift, it's heaven's
    great prize.
Go in peace, and know it's so.
Then, with clear heart, stand,
    arise,
And bless Fate's almighty blow.

While Peter began St. Petersburg's construction and provided the vision for this grand city, the city's main structures were erected during the reigns of Anne (1730-41), Elizabeth (1741-62) and Catherine II (1762-96).

The Building of St. Petersburg

1. The legacy of Russian neoclassicism is most dramatically enshrined in this city. St. Petersburg provides one of the world's finest examples of city planning: broad boulevards, magnificent architecture, canals, squares, fountains and monuments. Eighteenth–century city-builders believed that the city should provide an environment which would inspire the dweller's nobler spirits, his reason, his contemplation. Thanks to good city planning, the 20th–century city resident should be able to orient himself by looking around and seeing identifiable squares, boulevards, and monuments.

2. St. Petersburg is built on the various islands of the Neva delta; it is crisscrossed by numerous bridges over various canals and rivulets. Its "showcase" island is Vasilevsky (Basil's) Island. The main street, located on the mainland of the city, is Nevsky Prospect.

3. The oldest large structure in St. Petersburg is the St. Peter and Paul

Fortress (1712-33) built by the Italian architect Domenico Trezzini. Built to defend St. Petersburg against naval invasions, it was never used for this purpose. Across the Neva from this complex of structures stands the golden-spired Admiralty (1806-23), Russia's symbol of naval power.

4. Many of St. Petersburg's buildings were designed by Italians, notably, Bartolomeo Rastrelli (1700-1771) and Carlo Rossi (1775-1849). These architects left their mark on the entire city. Rastrelli's palaces stand as colorful single units in garden settings. They include the Winter Palace, or Hermitage, and the fountain-encircled Peterhof, located 10 to 12 miles west of the city. Rastrelli's buildings tend to be ornate, displaying rococco characteristics. Rossi's constructions are more neoclassical and simple in nature. Many are large building complexes, rather than single structures, connected by archways, such as the buildings of the General Staff.

5. Other buildings in St. Petersburg include:

   a. St. Isaac's Cathedral (1840's) near Senate Square.
   b. Kazan Cathedral (1801-11) on Nevsky Prospect.
   c. The Stock Exchange (1806), patterned after the Parthenon, on the "arrow" of Basil's island.
   d. Leningrad University (1722), on Basil's island, built by Trezzini.

Modern Leningrad is seen in Russian culture as the city of the Bolshevik revo-

lution and also as a "hero-city," having
survived the 900-day blockade of World War
II. The Piskarev Cemetery, north of the city,
contains mass graves for over 600,000 bodies
of persons who died during this blockade.

Bartolomeo Rastrelli. The Winter

Bartolomeo Rastrelli. The Peterhof Palace

Carlo Rossi. The General Staff
Headquarters. 1819-29.

St. Isaac's Cathedral. 1840s.

PUSHKIN

Aleksandr Sergeevich Pushkin (1799-1837) is considered by most Russians to be Russia's greatest poet. His contribution to the development of Russian literature and the Russian literary language is unique: no other writer influenced his culture so much in such a brief span of time.

Pushkin in Russian Literature

Pushkin's contributions to Russian literature are found in several areas:

1. His works helped "stabilize" the Russian literary language. The language of Pushkin's works set the norms for the vocabularies of many 19th—century Russian writers.

2. Pushkin's works "elevated" the quality of Russian writing. While set in Russian contexts (history, locations, legends), they deal with universal problems, such as love, jealousy, and alienation.

3. Pushkin's works helped set aesthetic standards for others to emulate, particularly in the area of lyric poetry. Even today, Russian poets are still compared to Pushkin.

4. Pushkin stands in Russian literary history as Russia's first great national poet.

Pushkin's Life

1. Pushkin was a nobleman, but his background was atypical. While tracing one part of his heritage to the most ancient of Russian families, he traced the other to Gannibal, a black man brought to Russia by Peter the Great. His Russian ancestry is mentioned in his play Boris Godunov; Gannibal is the main character in his uncompleted prose sketch, "The Arab of Peter the Great."

2. Pushkin was already writing verses in the lycee, many of them witty and off-color. As he matured, he also wrote longer, more serious works as well as drama and prose. He had many friends among poets of his day, and he was well-read in Western revolutionary and liberal thought. His independence and contempt made trouble for him with governmental authorities on numerous occasions. Happiness seemed to elude him. His marriage to a flirtatious and popular court woman, Natalie Goncharov, led to several scandals; the last of these resulted in a duel in which Pushkin was killed (January 29, 1837).

Stages in Pushkin's Works

Pushkin's works may be divided into four stages:

1. In his early period (until 1820), the young Pushkin experimented with various forms of verse writing, many of which are witty and frivolous. Some of these reflect his liberal and antiestablishment leanings. His mock fairy tale, Ruslan and Lyudmila (1819), was written during this period.

2. In his Byronic period (1820-24), Pushkin reflected the influence of the English poet. Pushkin's longer works are set in the Caucasus mountains and deal with "noble savages," who are not affected by the corruptions of the educated. His main work is Prisoner of the Caucasus (1822), which presents the reactions of a Russian nobleman held in captivity by Caucasian tribesmen. The contrast between educated and "primitive" values is likewise found in his Fountain of Bakhchisarai (1824), set in the Crimea.

3. In his maturing period (1824-30), Pushkin developed his own style. His main work is Eugene Onegin (1823-31), a novel-in-verse, which exposes the hypocrisies and hopes of the Russian aristocracy. The Gypsies (1827) returns to the "noble savage" theme, but this time, the issues are presented in a more complex, philosophical way. Poltava (1829) chronicles the defeat of the Swedes by Peter the Great.

4. His last, mature period (1830-37) was not as productive as his earlier ones; but in it he produced some of his best works, including several notable prose works: Tales of Belkin (1831), which are experiments in short story writing, and "Queen of Spades" (1834), a novella about a young man's lust for money. His long poem, The Bronze Horseman (1833), is about a downtrodden St. Petersburg civil servant who goes mad and has a vision of Falconet's statue of Peter the Great pursuing him.

Pushkin and the Genres of Literature

Pushkin's works set standards in Russian literature for many generations of writers. The genres in which Pushkin worked include:

1. <u>Lyric poetry</u>. Pushkin's numerous short "lyric" poems range from expressions of love to statements of political and moral conviction. His tender poems are sometimes touched with irony as in "I loved you once" (1829):

> I loved you once, and in my very
>   soul
> My love has not yet burnt out
>   dead.
> But I don't want alarm to sound
>   its toll
> And grieve by that which I have
>   said.
>
> I loved you, without words or
>   any sureness,
> First safely, then jealous to
>   the core.
> I first loved, with goodness and
>   with pureness,
> May God grant you're loved like
>   this once more.

Note the last line, "May God grant you're loved like this once more," underscores the poet's confidence that, despite the tenderness expressed, he knows his love will never be matched by anyone else's.

Pushkin's verse writing was always a difficult task for him, yet his works are characterized by an effortless style, as if one always talked in rhyme and meter. For this reason, some critics have termed Pushkin's verses as "perfect poetry."

2. The long story poem. One of Pushkin's favorite genres is the long story poem, usually set in some exotic location. Many employ Russian folk themes, some are in romantic Byronic settings, and still others are in mysterious, macabre situations. Pushkin, one of the first Russian writers to employ folk themes, has had many of his "tales" retold and "returned to the people" as original works of folklore. Ruslan and Lyudmila (1819) is a "reverse" fairy tale. It starts with the happy ending and then goes back into a quest for the heroine. All the elements of a good fairy tale are present, but they are presented in a surprisingly fresh way. Tsar Nikita and His Forty Daughters (1822) was inspired by a pornographic folk tale and was known by the aristocracy only in manuscript form. Tale of the Tsar Saltan (1831-34), written with much humor, has also become an opera by Rimsky-Korsakov.

3. The novel-in-verse. Pushkin's novel-in-verse, Eugene Onegin (1823-31), is for many critics the "first" modern Russian novel. In its form it is unique, written in rhymed stanzas that are deceptively simple. The plot is fairly uncomplicated. A young girl, Tatyana, falls in love with an older Petersburg dandy, Onegin, who is not interested in her. Later, he falls in love with her, but then she spurns him. Beneath this plot is a deep and penetrating look at Russian society at the turn of the 19th century. The heroine, Tatyana, is not the

"clinging vine" or the "idealized woman" found in the works of neoclassicism or romanticism. While being impressionable, she is also full of deep passions which are psychologically submerged. At the end of the novel, she admits to Eugene that she still loves him, but as a married woman, she cannot become involved in an affair.

Eugene Onegin, a dandy and a fop, bases his entire life on fashions and style. He senses that life has a deeper meaning but fails to find it, drifting from one intrigue to another. The goodness which Tatyana's romantic inclinations ascribe to Onegin is not actually there, and she must mature before she can realize this fact. Despite her maturity, she still loves Onegin; but she knows that her other responsibilities--to her husband and family--prevent her from going off with him.

4. Prose. Pushkin wrote a number of prose works. Most are written in a simple language, lacking the metaphoric images of his lyrics and the wit of his long poems. The Tales of Belkin (1831) comprise a group of short stories with "twist" endings. Captain's Daughter (1836) is a prose novel about the Pugachev rebellion. "Queen of Spades" (1834) is a novella concerning a young fortune-hunter who seeks to learn a secret "formula" for betting at cards.

5. Drama. Pushkin wrote one long historical drama, Boris Godunov (1825-31), in imitation of Shakespeare's "historical" plays. His "Little Tragedies" (1830) are short plays dealing with philosophical problems. One of them, "Mozart and Salieri," explores the

meaning of "genius." Salieri, a good musician who works slowly over his compositions, discovers that he cannot compete with the young Mozart, who simply dashes off symphonies. In the end, Salieri gets revenge on Mozart by poisoning him.

To this day, Pushkin's legacy lives. To many Russians he is as alive today as he was 150 years ago. His works are memorized, quoted and read many times over.

ROMANTICISM

Romanticism is a multifaceted term which refers to matters emotional, irrational and natural, rather than logical, reasonable and man-made. The variants of romanticism are so many that one critic once suggested that the term be used in the plural, i.e., "romanticisms."

Romanticism in Europe represented rebellion against the artificial rules of neo-classicism. Rising nationalism, an interest in exotic places, and a discovery of the common man all demanded new forms of artistic expression.

From Neoclassicism to Romanticism

During the late 18th century, some Russian works emerged which were termed "sentimentalist." Sentimentalism, frequently confused with romanticism, concentrated primarily on the emotions. Sentimentalist literature exploited the readers' feelings by depicting dark villains, pure heroines and bright heroes in contrived situations. Despite its shortcomings, sentimentalism began presenting emotions as legitimate subjects for literary presentation. In Russia, two sentimentalist works were extremely popular:

1. Aleksandr Radishchev's Journey from Petersburg to Moscow (1790). Patterned after Laurence Sterne's A Sentimental Journey through Europe, but lacking the humor of the English work, this semifictional work attempted to show the humanity of Russian land-bound peasants.

2. Nikolai Karamzin's "Poor Liza" (1792). This short story resembles many European sentimentalist works, notably Richardson's Pamela. Karamzin's hero is a commoner who falls in love with a nobleman. The nobleman seduces her and then marries another woman. Liza commits suicide by drowning in a Moscow pond.

Romanticism

Russian romanticism grew out of sentimentalism but had its own peculiarities. It concentrated on the personal experience, on the relationship of the self (the artistic "I") to its surroundings. Also, Russian romanticism explored lesser-known sides of Russia. Authors, artists and sculptors were interested in former times, faraway places, pantheism (the relationship of man to nature as a force in his life), and nationalism. In music, the first modern Russian composers accented the emotional and the nationalistic in their melodies.

The cultural heritage left by Russian Romanticism is strongly felt even in today's Russian culture.

1. Romanticism in Russian literature lasted from 1800 until 1830, and this period has been called Russia's "Golden Age" of poetry. Poets of this period include Aleksandr Pushkin, Mikhail Lermontov, and Evgeny Baratynsky. In the 18th century, literature was subordinated to architecture and science; in the 19th century the situation was reversed. Writers began to be regarded as "wise men" and "prophets," and no social

event was complete without a writer present. Theater-going (for the sake of the play and to see who else attended) became the favorite pastime of society. The "literary section" in various monthly journals became the most popular part.

2. In the fine arts, romantic painting treated natural scenes of faraway places (A. A. Ivanov's Monte Savelli), of peasant scenes (Venetsianov's Reapers and Sleeping Shepherd), and of legendary events (Bryullov's Last Day of Pompeii, Bruni's Death of Camelia, Sister of Horace). Even portraits were done with more emotionally-charged lines (swirls in clothing, drapery) than during the neo-classical period. Romanticism in Russian painting lasted from the 1800s to the 1840s.

3. In architecture, there were no equivalents to the great neoclassical building projects of the 18th century. The most significant buildings of the 19th century, the Bolshoi theater in Moscow and St. Isaac's Cathedral in St. Petersburg, were constructed in the classical style.

4. The music of 19th-century Russia is strongly nationalistic, using numerous folk motifs orchestrated according to the traditions of western Europe. Mikhail Glinka (1804-1857) attempted to create some operas on popular Russian themes, particularly Pushkin's "folk" poems. In the West, Peter Ilyitch Tchaikowsky (1840-93) is considered to be Russia's greatest national composer, although in Russia he was seen as something more of a westernizer. Nevertheless, many of his works employ folk themes.

The Social Situation During
the Period of Romanticism

Romanticism parallels a period of significant changes in the Russian nation. From an "also-ran" nation in the eyes of the rest of the world, Russia emerged as "the savior of Europe" after Napoleon's defeat in 1812. Democratic thought penetrated the noble intelligentsia and led to talk of reforms and of constitutional monarchy. The culmination of liberal thinking was an uprising in December 1825 called the "Decembrist Uprising." The young Nicholas I crushed the uprising, and many of the noblemen and literary figures who participated in it were arrested and exiled. This uprising marked the beginning of a split between the intellectuals and the government officials, a split which still exists today.

Mikhail Lermontov and the Caucuses

During this period, numerous writers travelled throughout Europe and to the Caucasus Mountains, which began to appear in their works as a locale for their stories and paintings. Italy, with its rich traditions, gentle climate and general friendliness, became particularly attractive to Russians, serving as a refuge for writers, such as Gogol, Gorky, Blok, and painters, such as A. A. Ivanov (Monte Savelli, 1850s), and Bryulov (Last Day of Pompeii, 1833).

The Caucuses, to which many Russian dissident writers were sent in exile to serve in the military, became the canvas for numerous stories and poems. Bestuzhev – Marlinsky's novel, <u>Ammalat Bek</u> (1832); several of Pushkin's long poems, "The Fountain of Bakhchisarai," "Prisoner of the Caucuses"; and works of other writers are set in this area, usually presenting the native Caucasians as possessing an element of the "truth" that "city people" (i.e. the Russians visiting there) do not have.

Caucasian settings are best known from the works of Mikhail Lermontov (1814-41). Despite his short life, many consider him on a par with Pushkin. Lermontov best exemplifies the image of the alienated poet.

Lermontov is reputed to have been descended from the Scots; one of his ancestors was supposed to have been the 13th-century bard, Thomas the Rhymer. He was born on October 15, 1814; in his twenty-seven years of life, he survived three ill-fated romances, numerous personal disputes, and several exiles. In his poetry, he looked for a world that does not exist on earth--a quest typical for romantic poetry. In the poem "The Angel," he states that the vision of the "better life" is given to the soul before birth but that, during its life, the soul does not find this better life anywhere on earth.

Lermontov's exile in the area of Pyatigorsk (North Caucuses) provided him with the setting for his novel <u>Hero of Our Times</u>. The main character, Pechorin, is anything but a traditional hero: he is distant, cruel, and insensitive to the needs of others; time and time again, he causes the destruction of those whom he encounters.

Like his heroes, Lermontov found life
boring and unchallenging. He expresses his
restlessness in the poem, "The Sail":

. . . The waves are playing, wind
    is snappy,
The mast is creaking o'er the
    seas,
Alas! It isn't happy,
And not from happiness it flees!
Below a streak of azure forms,
Above a ray of sun is sent.
But it, tormented, asks for
    storms,
As if in storms, one finds
    content!

In 1841, near Pyatigorsk, Lermontov got
into an argument with a Major Martynov.
The argument led to a senseless duel; and at
the age of 27, Lermontov was left bleeding
to death at the place where he was shot.

Nationalism

Before the 19th century, Russian society
was enamored of everything French. Indeed,
the nobility spoke more French than Russian
in their homes. However, the Napoleonic
invasion in 1812 resulted in much anti-French
feeling. One writer, Rastopchin, wrote:

. . . What kind of people are the
French? They're not worth a
kopeck! They're not worth either
looking at or talking about. In any
Frenchman's head you'll find only
windmills, hospitals and insane
asylums. Look at what these devils

have done in the past twenty years! They've chopped off heads like cabbages and have called everyone else evil. They call this equality and freedom and no one can open his mouth or thumb his nose at them.

The figure of Napoleon, personifying all that was evil in French society, was later satirized by Leo Tolstoy in <u>War and Peace</u>.

Anti-French feeling led also to a patriotism and nationalism that Russia had not seen before. Recalling the times when Moscow was called the "Third Rome," a new movement called "Pan-Slavism" emerged. It was encouraged by the autocratic government, which hoped that all Slavic nations would be united under Russia's direction.

In music, Tchaikowsky's <u>Marche Slave</u> was dedicated to this idea, as was his <u>1812 Overture</u>.

Gogol has been placed in many different writing camps: realist, symbolist, surrealist, naturalist, social critic, reactionary, and satirist. He is known for his brilliant dialogues and descriptions, for his earthy language, for his startling comparisons, and most of all for his tremendous humor. Many Russians are able to quote passages from Gogol's works, even though these passages are in prose rather than poetry.

Gogol was the first Russian author to use the everyday language; his interest in the comic, trivial, and unimportant and his attempt to romanticize and glorify the dull and lusterless have made him a poet of the commonplace.

Life and Works

Nikolai Gogol was born in the Ukraine in the town of Sorochintsy, in 1809. He studied in a gymnasium in the Ukraine and then moved to St. Petersburg in 1828. As a young man, he tried many different careers; he tried acting but failed in that venture. He then wrote a long narrative poem, Hanz Kuchelgarten (1829). He published it at his own expense; but then, fearing ridicule, he bought back many of the copies.

He ventured on a trip to the West but got only as far as Lubeck. Then he tried teaching, first, at the Patriotic Institute for Girls in St. Petersburg, then as an Assistant Professor of History at the University of St.

Petersburg. Turgenev recalls his brief career in the University:

> His teaching, to tell the truth, was done in a most original manner. First of all, Gogol usually skipped two lectures out of three. Secondly, even when he did appear at the faculty, he didn't speak, but rather whispered something completely incoherent and showed us small pictures of Palestine and other eastern lands. He was always confused. We were all convinced (and we were rarely wrong) that he didn't know anything about history . . . . At the final exam in his subject, he just sat there, bandaged in a handkerchief, as if from a toothache, and didn't open his mouth . . . I see him as if he were still before me: his thin long-nosed face wearing two highly protruding ends of a silk kerchief, which looked like ears.

When stories taken from Ukrainian folklore became popular in St. Petersburg, Gogol saw his chance to make some money in writing. He wrote a collection of stories based on Ukrainian folk motifs, called Evenings on a Farm Near Dikanka (1831-32). The publication met with great success, and Gogol's name as a writer became famous overnight.

Other short stories, using the same motifs, appeared two years later as Mirgorod (1835). In this collection, Gogol introduced some nonlegendary stories as well.

Taras Bulba, a short romantic novel about the battles between the Cossacks and Poles in the 17th-century Ukraine, is included in this collection. A third collection, Arabesques (1835), presented short stories set in St. Petersburg. In several of the stories, Gogol depicted Petersburg life as nightmarish and influenced by black powers.

Other works ensued. The play The Inspector General, produced in 1836, was a huge success. The Tsar was reputed to have said, "Well, everyone caught it in this play, but me, the worst of all." In 1842, he wrote his short story masterpiece, "The Overcoat."

In 1842, Gogol published the first part of a sort of "Divine Comedy," inspired by Dante--Dead Souls. The story involves a rogue, Chichikov, who travels around Russia buying up the names of dead serfs, who as "property" could be mortgaged for money.

As with his other plans, however, this one went awry. Part I, "The Inferno," became a masterpiece of Russian literature. Part II, the "Purgatorio" did not fare as well; Gogol was unhappy with it and ended up burning some sections. Part III, the "Paradiso," was never written.

His last testament is a work entitled Selected Passages from a Correspondence with Friends (1847). This work is a collection of sermons espousing various conservative and reactionary causes and advocating autocracy and serfdom. A far cry from the lampooning of government officials in The Inspector General, it shocked many liberals who saw Gogol as a guiding light, including the critic

Vissarion Belinsky, whose friendship with the writer ended with this publication.

Gogol became increasingly morbid in his last years. In 1848, he made a pilgrimage to Palestine. He was disappointed with the Holy Land; and returning to Russia in a negative humor, he starved himself to death, in 1852.

Gogol's Style

Gogol's works may be divided into three groups: tales based on Ukrainian folklore, tales about "ordinary" people, and tales of the "fantastic." A common thread may be found in all three groups, revealing a battle between good and evil for man's soul. Some critics have observed that the "devil" (chort) is frequently more important to Gogol than are his heroes. Indeed, one often encounters passages where evil is presented: in his Ukrainian stories, the devil appears as a character; in others, he may be sensed symbolically in the events which confront the characters.

Gogol's devil is rarely the classical "Satan"; on the contrary, Gogol's devil is the shallow, petty devil of corruption--a stupid, mediocre creature which destroys man, not by some grand deed, but rather by forcing him to make small compromises with what is true, beautiful, and good.

Gogol's verbosity--his use of many words, lists, catalogues, and incidental remarks-- provides Russian literature with a rich treasury of images. For example:

What a wonderful coat has Ivan Ivanovich! The best! And what astrakhan! Phew, damn it, what astrakhan! Purple with a slight frost! I'll bet you God knows anything if you could find one like it on anyone else! For the love of God, look at it, especially when he begins to talk to someone; look from the side: what a tasty delight! You cannot describe it: velvet! silver! fire! Oh, my God! Nicholas the Wonder-Worker, God's favorite! Why don't I have such a coat? He got it sewn at that time when Agafya Fedoseevna wasn't yet taking her trips to Kiev. You remember Agafya Fedoseevna? She's the very one who bit off the assessor's ear.

The trivial details give insights into his characters. In the following passage, the description of Manilov's estate gives us insights into his soul:

The village of Manilovka could attract few by its locale. The manor house stood alone in an open place, that is, on a hill exposed to all the winds, no matter from where they would decide to blow. . . . Five or six birches were showing their sparsely leafed tops in little clumps somewhere. Under two of them stood a garden house with a flat green cupola, blue wooden columns, and a sign, "Temple of Solitary Meditation." Lower, there was a weed-covered pond which, by the way, isn't all that uncommon in the English gardens of Russian landowners. At the foot of this rise and part way up the same slope, grey log huts stood here and there in a dingy way, which our hero, for some unknown reason, immediately began to count and counted more than two hundred. Nowhere among them could one find a single tree or any kind of greenery; everywhere one's eye was struck with only logs. . . . Even the weather itself helped: the day was neither clear nor gloomy, but sort of light-grey, the kind found on old uniforms of garrison soldiers--the kind of soldiers, by the way, who are peaceful but, occasionally, not too sober on Sundays. The picture was completed by an extraordinary rooster, a herald of changing weather who, despite the fact that his head was pecked through up to the brain by other roosters, still crowed very loudly and even flapped its wings, which were as bedraggled as old straw matting.

Gogol revels in using literary devices, but for different reasons than other authors. He admired Homer's Iliad, and employed homeric similes (analogies with long descriptions) in many of his works. His most famous one appears in Dead Souls:

Having entered the hall, Chichikov had to squint for a minute because the glitter from the candles, lamps, and women's dresses was overwhelming. Everything was bathed in light. Singly and in groups, black frock coats flitted by like flies near a bright white lump of sugar during a hot July summer, when the old cook cuts and divides it into glittering pieces before an open window. The children all see it; they gather around it and follow the movements of her coarse hands with curiosity. As they raise the mallet, airborne squadrons of flies, lifted up by the light air, soar up boldly, like pompous landlords and, taking advantage of the old woman's poor eyesight and of the sun which further irritated her eyes, they strew themselves out over the dainty pieces, singly in some places and elsewhere in groups. Sated by a sumptuous summer which would have offered various dainty dishes anyway without anything else needed, they then fly not in order to eat, but simply to show themselves off, to stroll around on a piece of sugar, to rub either front or rear leg against the other, or to scratch them against their wings, or to stretch their front paws out and to rub them together over their heads, then to turn around and fly away only to return in new bothersome formations.

Likewise, Gogol is a master of "negative description":

Through the gates of an inn in the provincial town of NN rode a rather attractive spring-hung small carriage, the kind ridden in by bachelors, retired lieutenant colonels, captains, landowners who own one hundred peasant souls--in a word, by all those who are known as gentry of average means. In the carriage sat a gentleman who was not a dazzler, nor was he of a homely appearance; he wasn't too fat, nor too thin. You couldn't say he was old; however, it wasn't possible to call him young, either. His arrival did not create any kind of noise in the town, nor was it accompanied by anything unusual; only two Russian peasants standing in the doorway of a tavern across the street from the inn managed to make some remarks dealing more, by the way, with the carriage than with its occupant: "Look at that," said one to the other, "Now that's a wheel for you! What do you think: if it had to, could that wheel make it to Moscow or not?" "It could," answered the other. "But to Kazan, I don't think it'll make it to Kazan." "No, it won't make it to Kazan," answered the other. And with this, the conversation ended.

Gogol then proceeds to discuss in great detail a passer-by who is never mentioned again in the novel.

Gogol greatly influenced Russian literature and left a legacy of humor, original images, and vivid characterizations.

GLINKA AND TCHAIKOWSKY

Modern Russian orchestral music dates from the middle of the 19th century. Eighteenth-century Russian music was imported from the West; Empress Anne brought in an Italian composer, Francesco Araja (1700-70), to write Italian operas in Russia.

Glinka

Mikhail Glinka (1804-57) is considered to be Russia's "first" modern composer. Glinka combined in his music two traits which were to prevail in Russian orchestral music throughout the century: Russian national themes and Western European orchestration techniques. Glinka's works include orchestral pieces, operas, and songs.

1. A Life for the Tsar or Ivan Susanin (1835-36), an opera, is based on a story from the Russian "time of troubles" (early 17th century). A Russian, Ivan Susanin, is captured by the invading Poles and instructed to lead them to a certain monastery where the Tsar is in hiding. Susanin, however, leads them astray, knowing that they will ultimately kill him when they learn of his deception. Folk songs are orchestrated throughout the opera.

2. Ruslan and Lyudmila (1838-42), an opera, is based on Pushkin's story-poem. The music is crisp and witty, but the libretto lacks the humor of Pushkin's original. In several parts, Glinka attempts to write

grotesque music (such as in "March of Chernomor"), incorporating some non-traditional combinations of musical instruments.

3. Kamarinskaya (1848) is based on a famous Russian folk dance. Glinka had previously orchestrated folk themes (including Spanish ones in 1844), but Kamarinskaya is one of his most successful attempts at this.

Tchaikowsky

Peter Ilyitch Tchaikowsky (1840-93) is the best known of all Russian composers in the West. His compositions employ European orchestrations and Russian folk themes. To many Russians of his time, he was considered a "Western" composer under the influence of Liszt, Wagner, and others.

Tchaikowsky's life was a tragic one. He was a homosexual and had deep fits of depression. In 1877 he married a woman he did not love and attempted to commit suicide. His innermost thoughts were shared in letters to Nadezhda von Meck, a woman he never met. His numerous works include:

1. First Symphony (1868), Second Symphony (Little Russian--Ukrainian) (1872), and the Third Symphony (1875), which are not considered as well-written as his last three. Recently, however, some critics have rediscovered original and skillfully created sections.

2. Piano Concerto #1 in B Flat Minor (1874). Although Nicholas Rubenstein,

Tchaikowsky's mentor, considered this work a disaster, it · has nevertheless become a traditional virtuoso concert performance piece.

3. <u>Fourth Symphony</u> (1877) and <u>Eugene Onegin</u> (1877). It is difficult to comprehend how one person could write a major symphony, a major opera, <u>and</u> a major ballet (see below) in one year, but Tchaikowsky did exactly this. All works are characterized by numerous memorable melodies. One of the criticisms of <u>Eugene Onegin</u> is that the orchestral parts are more interesting than the vocal ones.

4. <u>Swan Lake</u> (1877). Today, Russian ballet is closely associated with Tchaikowsky's ballet. The German legend of the tormented love of an enchanted swan-princess may symbolize the composer's own tragic life.

5. <u>Capriccio Italien</u> (1879) and <u>1812 Overture</u> (1880), both less serious works, use folk themes. The <u>Capriccio</u> was written after a trip to Italy and uses many Italian songs. The <u>1812 Overture</u> was designed for a performance outside the square of the Moscow Cathedral of the Savior. The work employs a "musical rivalry" between two national themes, the French "Marseillaise" and the Russian "God Save the Tsar."

6. <u>Sleeping Beauty</u> (1890) and <u>Nutcracker Ballet</u> (1892) are also based on German folk themes. Each is known for certain melodic sections. Most critics agree that <u>Nutcracker</u> is not on a par with Tchaikowsky's other ballets.

7. Fifth Symphony (1888) and Sixth Symphony (1893), his last two symphonies, are his greatest works. The Fifth Symphony has an inner dynamism which may be interpreted as a musical representation of "fate." The Sixth Symphony is seen by some as Tchaikowsky's own requiem. With the exception of the second movement, which is a bold scherzo, the work is pessimistic and subdued. Of particular beauty is the third movement, written in an off-balance 5/4 beat.

THE FIVE

Following the death of Nicholas I, Russia underwent a general spiritual reawakening. In music, this new spirit was evident in the work of a group called Moguchaya kuchka (literally, "the mighty handful") or "The Five." Consisting of Mili Balakirev, Cesar Cui, Modest Mussorgsky, Aleksandr Borodin and Nikolai Rimsky-Korsakov, this circle of composers considered themselves Russian nationalists whose goal was to explore and present Russia's musical heritage in the symphonic repertoire. Of these, four will be discussed here--Cui has not remained as well known as the others.

Balakirev

1. The mentor of this group, Mili Balakirev (1837-1910), was influential in the lives of many Russian composers. By 1857, Balakirev had begun to interest like-minded composer friends in his theories of an indigenous Russian orchestral repertoire. None, except Balakirev himself, was solely a composer: Cesar Cui was a young officer in the Army Engineer Corps; Modest Mussorgsky, a regimental officer; Nikolai Rimsky-Korsakov, a naval midshipman; Aleksandr Borodin, a chemist.

2. Balakirev's best works employ Russian and Oriental folk themes. Islamey uses melodies from the Caucuses. Originally a piano work, it was later orchestrated. Balakirev also wrote numerous "romances" based on the works of famous poets. His

interest in orchestrating Russian folk songs is best heard in the <u>Overture on Russian Folk Themes</u>, which employs four different songs.

Borodin

1. Balakirev's accomplishments, however, have not stood the test of time as well as those of Aleksandr Borodin (1833-87). Borodin, a scientist-artist who was interested in both chemistry and music, brings to his works the same kind of admiration for detail that he must have brought to his laboratory. Rimsky-Korsakov recalls that he was as likely to see him in the laboratory as behind the piano.

2. Borodin composed extremely slowly. His <u>First Symphony</u> took over five years to write. It was presented before the public on January 16, 1869. This symphony established his reputation as a major composer in Russia, but it is rarely played beyond the borders.

3. His <u>Second Symphony</u> was presented in Petersburg on February 26, 1877. In this work, Borodin was already interested in presenting some of the old Slavic themes, particularly those which may have been sung by the ancient troubadors. When compared with Balakirev's music, Borodin's works are considered to be more melodic.

4. Under the influence of Franz Liszt, Borodin wrote the symphonic poem <u>In the Steppes of Central Asia</u>. This work has the following note:

In the monotonous sandy steppe of Central Asia, we first hear the alien refrain of a quiet Russian song. The beat of horse and camel hooves is heard as they come closer. Then we hear the refrain of a mournful Eastern song. Along the limitless plain a native caravan is passing, guarded by Russian soldiers. It is making its long path faithfully and without fear under the protection of the Russian armed forces. The caravan passes further and further away. The peaceful refrains of the Russian and native songs merge into one unified harmony, the echoes of which remain for a long time in the steppe and finally die away in the distance.

5. Borodin's major work is the opera Prince Igor. In 1869, the art critic Stasov introduced the idea that Borodin should write an opera on the Igor Tale, and the idea remained with Borodin for the rest of his life. He spent a good part of twenty years compiling the various melodies and songs for this opera and never completed it. It was first performed on November 4, 1890, in an orchestration put together by Rimsky – Korsakov and Aleksandr Glazunov. The opera is not performed frequently outside Russia; however, the ballet sequence is often played as an orchestral piece, "The Polovtsian Dances."

Mussorgsky

Modest Mussorgsky (1839-81) is probably Russia's most "original" composer of the 19th century. Today his works appear modern and contemporary; in his own day, they were frequently regarded as incompetent, freakish, and dissonant. He is known primarily for his opera Boris Godunov and the piano suite Pictures at an Exhibition. However, he also managed to inspire the other members of "The Five" with his spirit of experimentation; in return, the others--notably Rimsky - Korsakov--helped him orchestrate several of his works.

Mussorgsky's biography reveals his deep family roots in Russian culture as well as his own psychological struggles.

1. Mussorgsky came from an ancient Russian family which traced its lineage to the Rurik princes of Kiev. Born and raised in the field and woods region of the Russian provinces, the young Mussorgsky heard and absorbed much of the folk and church music around him.

2. When he was of age, he enrolled in Cadet School in St. Petersburg, planning to become an Army officer. Nevertheless, he retained his interest in music, took piano lessons, and met the Russian composers of the day, notably, Borodin, Dargomyzhsky, and Balakirev. Balakirev took him in as a pupil and encouraged him to develop his own style of composing.

3. Mussorgsky, like Gogol and to some extent Dostoevsky, experienced great difficulty in living in the St. Petersburg environment and underwent several morbid crises in the 1860s and '70s. One manifestation of these crises was alcoholism.

4. Nevertheless, Mussorgsky produced the skeletons of numerous works which were later orchestrated by his friends of "The Five." Mussorgsky died in 1881 while trying to complete two operas, Khovanshchina and Sorochinsky Fair.

Mussorgsky's style is the most distinctive of all the composers of the 19th century. Unlike most of Tchaikowsky's works, Mussorgsky's melodies are contorted; his rhythms are varied and highly unusual.

1. It was formerly believed that he was very much under the influence of "The Five." Now, however, it is much more evident that his work was uniquely his own.

2. The main influence on Mussorgsky was folk music; but it affected him differently than it did Rimsky-Korsakov, Balakirev, or Borodin. Mussorgsky's music is "folklike" in that it uses the melodic progressions and harmonic patterns and rhythms of folk music. Rarely, however, does Mussorgsky employ actual folk melodies in his music.

3. Mussorgsky was interested in "realism" in music. He wrote about his intention to present rhythm and melody in terms of voice patterns, intonations, and psychological moods.

Some of Mussorgsky's works include:

1. Songs and Dances of Death (1857-77), music written to a cycle of poems by Golenishchev-Kutuzov. Through these songs, Mussorgsky attempts to capture the poet's satanic moods in new rhythms and melodic progressions that resemble human speech.

2. <u>Song of the Flea</u> (1879). This comic song about how a king knights a flea has become a virtuoso piece for bassos.

3. <u>Night on Bald Mountain</u> (1867). This work is one of Mussorgsky's few completed orchestral pieces. Mussorgsky orchestrates an imagined "witches' sabbath," perhaps inspired by one of Gogol's early short stories, and by legends of witches in the Kiev area.

4. <u>Pictures at an Exhibition</u> (1874). This piano piece is now more famous in its orchestration by Ravel. It was written on the occasion of the death of an artist friend, Viktor Hartmann, whose works were put together in an exhibition after his death. Selections in this work are musical descriptions of the art works. They include:

a. "Promenade," a leitmotif which occurs throughout the work, representing the "strolling" of the beholder from one picture to the next.

b. "Gnomus," a rhythmically and harmonically contorted work expressing the prancing about of an elf.

c. "Bydlo," the Polish oxcart, which portrays the swaying of an oxcart on an uneven country road.

d. "The Hut of the Baba-Yaga," a musical expression of the Russian witch's house on chicken legs which is able to turn when magic words are spoken.

e. "The Great Gate of Kiev," which uses the "Promenade" theme in a procession-like manner, together with fanfares, drumbeats and bells, to evoke the images of medieval Kiev.

5. "Boris Godunov" (1870-74). Of his several operatic attempts, Mussorgsky is famous for one, "Boris Godunov." This massive work, the most popular of all Russian operas, interweaves Mussorgsky's distinctive rhythmic and melodic style with the words of Pushkin's play depicting the well-known legend that Boris Godunov killed the legitimate heir to the Russian throne, Tsarevich Dmitry, in order to become Tsar.

Rimsky-Korsakov

Nikolai Rimsky-Korsakov (1844-1908) served as the "orchestrator" of "The Five." As a musical scholar, he employed numerous folk themes and rhythms in his orchestral and operatic works. His music, tuneful and easy on the ears, is often based on national folk themes. The operas are rarely presented beyond Russian borders because of their local character; for the most part they have not been translated from the Russian and are not as highly regarded as are the works of Mussorgsky or Tchaikowsky. Yet, they retain a charm of their own, a lightness which is typical of this composer.

1. Scheherezade (1887-88) is an orchestral suite expressing some of the Tales from the Arabian Nights. His mastery over orchestration may be witnessed in the first movement, entitled "The Sea and Sinbad's Ship," a variation-on-a-theme. It is conceived in such a way that one is only remotely

conscious of seemingly endless repetitions of only a few bars of music. Scheherezade is probably Rimsky-Korsakov's most frequently performed work.

2. Tale of the Tsar Sultan (1899-1900) is based on Pushkin's story-poem. This opera uses old Russian folk songs and dances already familiar to the Russian audience. The most famous section of this opera is the "Flight of the Bumblebee."

3. Overture on Liturgical Themes (1888), better known as the Russian Easter Overture, combines both pagan and Christian melodies and rhythms, attempting to express man's joy at the return of spring. As Rimsky-Korsakov wrote:

> Does not the prancing and fro-licking of the Biblical King David before the ark express a feeling of the very same order as that of the idol-worshipper's dance? Isn't the Russian Orthodox bell-chime the best thing for instrumental church dance music? Aren't the shaking beards of the white-garmented and surpliced priests and deacons singing "Beautiful Easter" in the tempo of allegro vivo, etc.; don't they carry your imagination away to pagan times? And what about those paskha-cheese and Easter kulich cake dishes and the lit candles?--how far away is all of this from Christ's teachings! This is what I wanted to reproduce in my overture: the entire legendary and pagan side of the holiday, this

transition from the somber and mysterious evening of Holy Saturday to the somewhat unbridled pagan-religious joy of Holy Easter morning.

Throughout the work, bells provide a light, rhythmic counterpoint to the solemn church hymns, creating a joyous, colorful musical interpretation of the Easter rite.

REALISM

One of Russian culture's great contributions to world literature is the "realistic" novel. Indeed, the period 1840-1917 represents a long affair of Russian artists and writers with the realistic tradition. Realism is found not only in literature; it is also found in the visual arts. One composer, Modest Mussorgsky, even attempted to capture the spirit of realism in music.

The term "realism" implies that art presents life "as it really is," rather than as an artist interprets it subjectively. Unlike romantic art, which tries to communicate the innermost feelings and emotions of a person, realistic art presents how those feelings are expressed outwardly. The realistic artist attempts to stand a bit to one side of the experience he is describing and allow the beholder to deal with it on his own terms.

Of course, it is difficult to present life "as it really is"--in fact probably more difficult than to convey feelings. The realistic artist still needs to select the episodes he wishes to describe and must rely on specific devices to convey the illusion that he is presenting "reality." Realistic works, after all, are still products of the imagination.

Due to the length of the period of realism as well as the breadth of works which could be called "realistic," we have divided the tradition into two parts: the earlier "objective" tradition and the later "critical" or "psychological" one.

Objective Realism

"Objective" realism attempts to convey reality with the least amount of "interference" from the author/narrator. To do this, many realistic artists relied on specific devices. Some of the more common are:

1. The use of detail. Realistic art concentrates on the details of experience rather than on grand generalizations. In discussing this process Chekhov wrote:

> . . . on the dam glistens the neck of a broken bottle, by the shadow of a mill-wheel. Suddenly, you have a moonlit night, all ready.

2. Presentation of a "slice of life." The realistic work does not need to have a formal beginning or end. On the contrary, the writer may wish to have the reader look into a particular situation which is already underway. Events may have happened in the story before the novel began; likewise, the story may continue after the novel's last page.

3. The background or "social setting." The social setting, translated into Russian as "byt," plays a significant role in Russian realistic works. It provides the literary "canvas" on which the story unfolds. All characters are subjected, in varying degrees, to the customary ways "things are done," to the value systems and beliefs of the others around them.

4. Nature descriptions. Nature, in realistic works, frequently underscores the human condition; i.e., if a "stormy" relationship exists between two persons, a storm might be gathering somewhere in the distance.

5. Believable dialogue. Realistic writing heavily depends on accurate and believable dialogue. Numerous Russian realistic writers re-created the actual dialogue of persons of various social levels by using words which are not from "literary" or "standard" Russian. Characters may be given peculiar dialogue traits to help further identify them.

Objective Realism in Literature

1. Ivan Turgenev (1818-83) is the most outstanding representative of this type of writing. His works are universally acclaimed as masterpieces of detached writing. He rarely reveals his own prejudices; rather, the reader is left to make his own conclusions. His most famous works include Sportsman's Sketches (1847-51), Rudin, On the Eve (1860), and Fathers and Sons (1862). (See the separate section on Turgenev for greater detail.)

2. Alexei Pisemsky (1820-81). Pisemsky is also a craftsman of the realistic art. The narration in his novel A Thousand Souls (1858) is almost cruelly detached from the various problems of his main character, Kalinovich, who seems to want to destroy himself after he has achieved social success. His play A Bitter Fate (1859) is a masterpiece of tragedy focused upon the demise of a proud but offended Russian peasant.

3. Ivan Goncharov (1812-91), is famous for his novel <u>Oblomov</u> (1869). The novel is a character study of a Russian "type" who sees no reason for pursuing an active life, choosing instead to remain in bed. Later, the character of Oblomov became a symbol for Russian inactivity; and the term "Oblomovitis" was coined by the radical critic, Nikolai Dobrolyubov, to refer to such a condition.

4. Sergei Aksakov (1791-1859) wrote several works depicting rural society. His most famous works, including <u>Years of Childhood</u> (1858), are reminiscences.

5. Alexander Ostrovsky (1823-86) was one of Russia's few 19th-century professional playwrights. Author of over 50 plays, his works depict merchant and bourgeois society. Some of his more famous include <u>The Storm</u> (1860), <u>The Forest</u> (1871), <u>The Dowery-less Girl</u> (1879).

Objective Realism in the Fine Arts

Russian realistic paintings are devoted to landscape painting, portraiture, or the depiction of some historical event. Some of the more noted ones include:

1. Ivan Aivazovsky: <u>The Ninth Billow</u> (1850), <u>Wave</u> (1889)

2. Vasily Perov: <u>The Last Tavern</u> (1868)

3. Grigory Myasoedov: <u>The reading of the manifesto of Feb. 19, 1861</u>

4. Aleksandr Ivanov: Water and Stones (1850s)

5. Ivan Shishkin: Pines, Illumined by the sun (1886), Ship-timber Meadow (1898)

6. Fyodor Vasiliev: Abandoned Windmill (1872-73)

7. Ivan Kramskoi: Portrait of Mina Moiseev (1882)

Psychological or Critical Realism

"Psychological" or "critical" realism was created by writers such as Fyodor Dostoevsky, Leo Tolstoy, Mikhail Saltykov — Shchedrin, the poet Nikolai Nekrasov, several painters including Ilya Repin, and to some extent, composers like Modest Mussorgsky.

Dostoevsky and the Search Within

Fyodor Dostoevsky, throughout his mature career, explored the ramifications of intelligence and consciousness and came up with some insights regarding Russia and her future. His novels are a long, tortuous series of questions which raise more problems than they solve.

Dostoevsky's characters reflect upon what he considered the essential decision made by each person: for "freedom" on the one hand, or for "security" (or "happiness") on the other. Not only individuals, but governments make decisions for the one or the other. In his famous "Legend of the Grand Inquisitor" in The Brothers Karamazov, Dostoevsky hypothesizes a second coming of Christ during the time of the Spanish Inquisition. The Grand Inquisitor, who is confronted by Christ's presence, cynically tells Him that His presence is no longer needed on earth.

> No science will give them bread while they remain free. In the end, they will lay their freedom at our feet and will tell us, "Enslave us, but feed us." They will understand themselves that freedom and earthly bread enough for all are inconceivable, since never, never will they be able to divide it among themselves! We will deceive them again, since we will not let them come to Thee. In this deception will lie our suffering since we will have to lie.

To Dostoevsky, social reforms and programs are ultimately evil because they rob man of his freedom for the sake of some "common good." The difference between man and the other animals, insofar as he is concerned, is man's ability to make decisions, to actually will something evil for himself, if only to assert his individuality.

Russia, to Dostoevsky, was purer than either the Western or the Eastern nations. Untouched by Western Christianity--which, to Dostoevsky, had sold out to materialism and, hence, the devil--Russia still had a hope of finding its own way in history and of being a sort of international "Christ," reconciling the nations of the world to one other.

Tolstoy and the
Search in the World

Leo Tolstoy also saw a unique strength in Russia emanating from the Russian people, who were untouched by city ways. It was through this mysterious interplay between the Russian land and the Russian people that the French were conquered. While the settings of his novels varied and Tolstoy hardened his views of morality, he still returned to the Russian peasant, who seemed to be closest to answers about the mysteries of life.

Tolstoy's desire to "go to the people" paralleled the so-called Populist or Narodnik movement, in which numerous intellectuals went to the countryside to help liberate peasants from their environment.

Other Writers

1. Nikolai Nekrasov (1821-77). A poet and editor of the liberal journal Sovremennik (The Contemporary) and later Otechestvennye zapiski (Notes from the Fatherland), Nekrasov decried the inequalities in Russian society in both articles and poetry. His long story-poems Frost, Red-Nose (1863) and Who Can Live Well in Russia? (1863-1877) combine liberal social commentary with images from Russian folklore.

2. Mikhail Saltykov-Shchedrin (1826-89). A novelist-satirist, he is best known for his novel The Golovlev Family (1876), an account of a decaying, hypocritical gentry family. The lack of any positive characters conveys a sense of gloom and foreboding; yet one senses

that some characters have a desire to escape from the world they have created.

The Wanderers

Paintings which were critical of Russian society and which often made social statements were created, for the most part, by a semiorganized group of painters called "The Wanderers." Initially rebelling against the standards set by the St. Petersburg Conservatory of Art, these painters took their exhibitions "to the people" by depicting recognizable scenes from Russian legends and history as well as from contemporary life. Many paintings were highly critical of Russian life. Numbered among the Wanderers were: Ilya Repin, G. G. Myasoedov, Ivan Kramskoi, Konstantin Savitsky, and N. A. Yaroshenko.

The critical realistic tradition, encouraged by the Wanderers, dominated Russian painting toward the end of the 19th century. Some of the more famous paintings include:

1. V. Perov's The Refectory (1876), depicting a monastery repast, is a cruel attack on the Orthodox church. The painting shows monks participating in an orgy of gluttony and womanizing while a statue of a crucified Christ is seen in the background.

2. K. A. Savitsky's The Meeting of the Icon (1878) and Repin's The Procession of the Cross in the Kursk Gubernya (1880-83) are but two pictures depicting the Russian masses in the provinces participating in religious events.

3. G. G. Myasoedov's The Reapers (1887), perhaps inspired by Tolstoy, idealizes the life of the peasant at his work.

4. Portraits were also painted by the critical realists. Repin's Mussorgsky (1881) captures the composer only days before his death--a victim of alcoholism and depression. Repin's Tolstoy the Ploughman (1887) shows the elderly writer participating in his favorite pastime, tending to his fields.

TURGENEV

Life and Works

Ivan Sergeevich Turgenev (1818-83) has been universally acclaimed as one of Russia's greatest realists. Indeed, when one discusses the term "realism" and especially the idea of "objective realism," Turgenev presents us with some of the best models in European prose. Life is presented "as it really is," with little fanfare and soul-searching. To other European writers of the realistic tradition, Turgenev was among the best. Henry James summarized their admiration by calling him "the novelist's novelist."

Born on October 28, 1818, Turgenev came from Russian nobility; his life spans many of the great events which affected Russia in the 19th century: the Decembrist uprising, the European revolutions of 1848, the freeing of the serfs, the assassination of Alexander II.

Turgenev began his advanced education in the University of Moscow in 1833; but after one year, he moved to St. Petersburg with his mother and enrolled at the University of St. Petersburg. Over the years, Turgenev met the other great Russian writers: Pushkin, Gogol, Tolstoy and Dostoevsky. Turgenev began his writing career by composing poetry, but he soon abandoned verse for prose. His inclination for the lyrical may be found in his many descriptions of nature.

In 1838 Turgenev travelled to Berlin where he met many Russian idealists and radicals. Their views during his three-year stay influenced many of his opinions, particularly regarding the abolition of serfdom and the desirability of the adoption of Western liberal ideas in Russia.

Turgenev returned to Russia in 1841, tried a career in the civil service which did not work out satisfactorily, and then turned to professional writing.

In 1845 he had a falling out with his dictatorial mother concerning his non-aristocratic way of life and his infatuation with the married singer, Pauline Viardot. Her marriage never appeared to bother Turgenev, and he frequently accompanied her on her tours. Other than his mother and Viardot, Turgenev had few women in his life.

In 1847 Turgenev wrote some short stories based on rustic themes. By 1852, these were compiled into a collection called Sportsman's Sketches. The stories humanized the Russian peasant--Radishchev had done this earlier in Journey from St. Petersburg to Moscow--and they were even regarded by some as threatening to the tsarist regime, which was threatened by numerous peasant uprisings. The work probably did play a small role in the abolition of serfdom in 1862. Alexander II is reputed to have read this collection and to have felt compassion for the serf as a fellow human being.

Turgenev's novels often treat contemporary Russian problems. In Rudin (1856), Turgenev studies a character who is eloquent and idealistic but who lacks strong commitment to any value. Rudin is incapable of responding to the love of a young woman and ends up dying on the Paris barricades in an empty attempt to find a purpose in life. At the same time, the reader is introduced to the life of the provincial Russian gentry, which is likewise characterized by lack of direction and emptiness.

In Nest of Gentlefolk (1859), Turgenev portrays the old gentry as having noble characteristics, despite the emptiness of their existence on estates far away from the capital. He typically avoids making caricatures out of his characters, no matter what their political and social views.

On the Eve (1860) portrays two new kinds of characters: a genuine revolutionary and a "new" woman, who is willing to break her bonds to her family to venture out on her own. Several critics noted ironically that Turgenev would make his "man of action" a Bulgarian rather than a Russian.

His best work is Fathers and Sons (1862) in which he contrasts the anticipations of two generations of Russian liberal society. The two representatives of these generations are Pavel Kirsanov, an old liberal, and Evgeny Bazarov, a younger "nihilist" who believes in nothing except science. Like other Turgenevian heroes, Bazarov cannot face the prospect of love; in the end, Bazarov perishes, and the circumstances of his death lead one to believe that he may have committed suicide.

Smoke (1867) presents an attack on class hierarchies in Russian society. Virgin Soil (1877) depicts idealistic young Russians in the Populist movement.

Disappointed with Russian backwardness, Turgenev finally emigrated to France in 1871. For the most part, he remained in exile after that year.   He died in Paris in 1883.

Turgenev's Style

Turgenev's style is not nearly as dramatic as that of Dostoevsky, nor is he as pedantic as Tolstoy.   Yet, he was "up-to-date" in his themes, discussing social issues and presenting characters who were at the cutting edges of social change.   In Turgenev's works, one encounters such subjects as: the emancipation of women, the humanity of the serf classes, the conflict of the generations, the Populist movement, and Pan-Slavic nationalism.

Turgenev's style is both romantic and realistic.   Turgenev's romanticism is found in some   of   his   characters   who   present themselves   as   mysterious   strangers   in   new environments.   Turgenev's realism emerges in his investigation of the true nature of his characters.   His probing puts him in touch with the details of life, those small bits of evidence   about   people   which   reveal   their nature.

Turgenev's style is likewise lyrical.   His narratives are interspersed with elaborate descriptions of nature--of the world which is beyond man's control but which comments upon the human situation.   Turgenev's world is that of the Russian provincial estate, inhabited   by   intelligent   yet   frequently unmotivated gentry as well as a broader mass of serfs and peasants.

For the most part, the social setting and the plot take second place to character study in Turgenev's works. His characters fall into definite categories. Some are:

1. <u>The superfluous man.</u> Many of Turgenev's heroes resemble this type of person--one who finds it difficult to fit into any society or social group. Usually of good intentions, the superfluous man is unable to convert his good feelings into any sort of action. This term, taken from the title of Turgenev's novella, "Diary of a Superfluous Man" (1850), is also used to describe similar characters in the novels of other Russian writers.

2. <u>The strong, purposeful woman.</u> Turgenev's women are strong, purposeful in their actions, and willing to commit themselves to relationships. In most instances, they cannot find a male who has enough strength to respond to them. Turgenev's older women are frequently matriarchs who lord their power over friends, servants and serfs.

3. <u>The dedicated also-ran.</u> Turgenev's novels also contain various characters who, while not possessing the outward flair of his superfluous heroes, nevertheless maintain a quiet dedication to their work and even serve as mediators between the superfluous man and others.

4. <u>Character-caricatures.</u> Turgenev presents many secondary characters as interesting "types" who possess some interesting and colorful trait. These characters, not as fully developed as others,

embellish and add a touch of humor to the various episodes.

Rudin and Themes in Turgenev's Works

Rudin (1856) is Turgenev's first novel. The "romantic" plot reveals a mysterious stranger who appears in a tranquil provincial setting. His appearance interrupts the boredom of the residents of the estates in this province. Rudin impresses everyone by his eloquence; but as the reader gets to know him better, he learns that Rudin is not the person he seemed to be at first.

The philosophical issues raised in the novel center on the relationship between the active and the contemplative life. Rudin is eloquent and extremely intelligent, but he cannot motivate himself to become committed to anything. His opposite, Lezhnev, is much less eloquent but quietly acts according to his convictions. The young Natalya Lasunskaya, who falls in love with Rudin, is willing to follow him to the ends of the earth; yet Rudin cannot respond to this act of love by the young woman.

The social world in Rudin is that of manorial, provincial Russia. The gentry, who do not need to work for a living, are well-educated yet bored since they encounter only a small circle of neighbors. Relations between people are dictated by an ethic of manners which keeps the uglier aspects of social life submerged under rituals of "gentility." This particular manorial world is dominated by Mme. Darya Mikhailovna

Lasunskaya (Natalya's mother), whose word is law. She is entertained by Rudin's eloquence and enjoys having him around; yet, when a notion arises that Rudin might marry her daughter, she lets Natalya know about her dissatisfaction. When Rudin hears about Darya Mikhailovna's feelings from Natalya, he decides to leave rather than commit himself to a struggle with the old woman.

The psychological issues deal with Rudin's inability to understand himself. Why is he unable to act or commit himself to anything? He never discovers the answer. At the end of the novel, he is killed on the barricades in Paris. Ironically, those who see him killed take him for a Pole.

DOSTOEVSKY

General Background

Even today, Fyodor Dostoevsky (1821-81) and his writings are steeped in controversy. Because of his conservative leanings, he is not published much in the USSR, although most Soviets know his major works. Elsewhere, Dostoevsky is published widely. Hollywood has made a film of Brothers Karamazov. Crime and Punishment and The Idiot were made into films in Western Europe as well as in the USSR.

One of the best ways to understand Dostoevsky is to confront the following passage from The Idiot. In it, Prince Myshkin is describing what goes through the mind of a person about to be beheaded at a public execution:

> Finally he began to go up the steps; his legs were tied together and had to move in tiny steps. The priest must have been an intelligent person; he stopped talking but continued to give him the cross to kiss. At the bottom of the steps he was very pale, and when he came up onto the scaffold he became as white as a sheet, completely white as writing paper. . . . It's strange that it's rare for people to faint during these final seconds! On the contrary, the head works and lives fiercely; it must be strong, strong like a machine at full steam. I imagine that various thoughts must

throb in the mind, all of them incomplete and perhaps even funny and irrelevant: thoughts like "look at that one staring at me, he has a wart on his forehead; there, that executioner has a lower button that is rusty," all the while knowing and remembering everything. There's that point which you cannot forget in any way, and it's impossible to faint, and everything near it, near this point, is moving and turning. And to think that this goes on until the last quarter second, when the head is on the block and it waits and . . . knows, and suddenly hears the iron clang above it! You'd definitely hear that! If I were lying there, I would listen for it on purpose and hear it! And imagine that to this day they argue that, perhaps, the head, even after it has been severed, knows that it has been severed. What a thought! And what if it knows this for five seconds!

The intensity of this experience, the probing into the very depths of consciousness appears to be at the center of all Dostoevsky's works. While this episode is imagined by the novel's hero, a similar one was actually experienced by Dostoevsky himself.

In 1848, a group of young radicals called the Petrashevsky Circle, including Dostoevsky, were arrested. Nicholas I considered all such groups dangerous, especially in a year when many revolutions were occuring in Western

Europe. Dostoevsky was sentenced to serve in exile as a private soldier for four years but was not told this fact; instead he was told that he was sentenced to death. At first, he was imprisoned in the Peter and Paul Fortress and finally was led out to be executed. He was reprieved as he was standing facing the guns of the firing squad. One of the other prisoners undergoing the same experience reportedly lost his mind. Dostoevsky keeps returning to this experience in his writings. At another point in The Idiot, he writes:

> To kill a man for murder is an incomparably worse punishment than the original crime. Killing by sentence is incomparably more horrible than getting killed by a robber. The man killed by robbers is stabbed at night in the woods and somehow always hopes that he'll be saved at the very last moment. . . . But in this case, this last hope, which makes it ten times easier to die, is removed completely. Here is the sentence, and in the very fact that you cannot escape it lies all the torment. There is no greater torment on earth. . . . Maybe there's a person somewhere who had been read his sentence and then was later told, "Go, you're forgiven." Maybe such a person could tell you about it. Even Christ has spoken about this torment and horror. No, you cannot treat a person this way!

Of course, the author is that "man" who could perhaps tell. The episode stresses the importance that Dostoevsky was to put on the idea of "consciousness" and "self-awareness" in his later works.

Life and Works

Fyodor Dostoevsky was born on October 30, 1821, into the family of a physician. His background was Ukrainian and Russian. A passionate literature buff even as a young man, he attended a Military Engineers' school; but despite studying for four years, he remained interested in literature. His early works include:

1. Poor Folk (1844-45) is a novel-in-letters. The liberal poet Nekrasov read it to his colleagues; one of them later proclaimed, "A new Gogol has arisen!" Indeed, Dostoevsky initiated the Gogolian style: wordiness, settings in the lower-class parts of St. Petersburg, and emphasis on the grotesque.

2. The Double (1846) was also written in the Gogolian style. This surrealistic work received a much cooler reception than did Poor Folk. In some ways, this work picks up the premise of "The Nose," except that now an entire "double" or other self of a man appears to be replacing the main character.

3. The Landlady (1847), A Weak Heart, and White Nights (1848) are works with somewhat mystical settings, perhaps a little over-sentimentalized (as Dostoevsky admitted doing in White Nights). In 1848 he began a novel, Netochka Nezvanova, but his arrest prevented him from completing it.

Many of Dostoevsky's thematic peculiarities were already evident in these early works: his interest in the downtrodden, in the helpless romantics who cannot change the world about them, in the city of St. Petersburg. The moral questions to be so profoundly raised in his later works are not strongly emphasized in these early attempts. Were Dostoevsky to have died before his exile, as his biographer E. H. Carr observes, these works probably would have been noted as "minor classics" which few people would have read.

4. Between 1848 and 1857, Dostoevsky wrote virtually nothing. He served out his penal servitude in Siberia, in Omsk, from January 1850 to January 1854. During this time his nervous consciousness, already aroused to the point of delirium at the mock execution, became focused upon the world, life, and the people of Russia. He studied the Bible and pondered the way the Russians accepted penal servitude--both the prisoners and the people of Siberia, who, from the "outside," endured the prisoners' suffering with them. His experiences were finally put together in semifictionalized form in 1862 as Notes from the House of the Dead, which discussed the questions of bondage just at the time that serfdom was abolished in Russia.

In prison, Dostoevsky contemplated humiliation, dignity, and freedom. He began to explore the possibility that there are parts of the human being that government, tyranny, and oppression cannot destroy. In House of the Dead, he writes:

. . . In general, the lower classes are irritated by any kind of sloppiness from on high, any kind of squeamishness shown them. Others think, for instance, that if a convict is fed well, taken care of and dealt with according to the law, that everything is fine once and for all. This is also an error. Every person, no matter who he is or how he has been humiliated, nevertheless either instinctively or unconsciously demands respect regarding his worth as a man. The convict knows himself that he is a convict, an outcast, and knows his place before the commander; but neither branding nor fetters will make him forget that he is a human being as well.

Dostoevsky also observed a peculiarity about the "order" of life in Russian society--an order which began to lead him to some conservative conclusions. In the same passage he continues:

> . . . the convicts themselves do not like to be treated too familiarly and such overly friendly treatment from their commander [merits their scorn]. They want to respect the commander; and if this happens, they cease respecting him.

Thus man, to Dostoevsky, needs both to be human and to understand his "place" in the world, in his society. As Dostoevsky's writing developed, he began to believe that Russia could provide a unique model of society for the entire world. Central was the need for God-like compassion between people, modelled on God's love for humanity.

Dostoevsky remained in Siberia until 1859; then he returned to St. Petersburg, where he began publishing a journal, Vremya (Time). After his return to St. Petersburg, he wrote what are considered his greatest works. Most of them were serialized; in order to keep the reader interested, the moments of greatest intensity were placed at the ends of chapters.

5. The Insulted and the Injured (1861) and House of the Dead (1862) both appeared in Vremya. In 1862-63, Dostoevsky travelled in Europe (and gambled--his chronic disease); he condemned the Western bourgeois society that he saw, and became a late "Slavophile" in Winter Notes on Summer Impressions.

6. In 1863, publication of Vremya journal ceased; it was subsequently continued as the journal Epoch. Dostoevsky experienced financial disaster while at the same time suffering from miseries caused by women and gambling; in addition, his wife died from tuberculosis, and his brother Mikhail, his partner in publishing, also died. Furthermore, he was suffering from epilepsy, and his illness was getting worse. It was at this time that he wrote Notes from the Underground, which presents a philosophical exposition of many of Dostoevsky's thoughts. In a sense, it is his introduction to his later novels; without this work, the others cannot be understood as well. The work presents an overview of how he treats these themes artistically.

The works which follow Notes from the Underground represent not only Dostoevsky's greatest achievements, but also some of the most profound novels written in any language during the nineteenth century:

7. <u>Crime and Punishment</u> (1865) explores the proposition that a person can take justice into his own hands. The novel is a detective story in which the killer, a young student who axe-murders an elderly landlady whom he considers a parasite on humanity, undergoes mental "punishment" for this crime until he finally confesses.

8. <u>The Idiot</u> (1869) deals with the premise that a Christ-like person could not survive in contemporary society. The character of Prince Myshkin, who is an epileptic (like Dostoevsky), is placed into conflict and contrasted with other characters in St. Petersburg society.

9. <u>The Possessed</u> (1871-72) represents Dostoevsky's attempt to satirize liberal reformers and radical students. In the novel, Dostoevsky shows how these characters disguise their hunger for power under various ideological trappings. One of the most bitterly satirized characters in the book represents Ivan Turgenev.

10. <u>A Raw Youth</u> (1875) is not one of Dostoevsky's better works; it has inspired little literary criticism over the years. The central character, Versilov, is one of Dostoevsky's most puzzling and mysterious—a character who believes in the need for societies and governments to be centered in God, yet at the same time manages to neglect his sensitive and growing son.

11. <u>The Brothers Karamazov</u> (1878-80) is the culmination of the ideas developed in Dostoevsky's earlier novels. In this work he explores the notion of sainthood, the role of

Russia in the world, the passions of man, consciousness, and the action of God in the world. Many critics consider this work Russia's greatest novel.

The Issues in
Notes from the Underground

At its most elementary level, Notes from the Underground is a rebuttal to a novel by the radical critic Nicholas Chernyshevsky, What Is To Be Done? which describes a fictionalized utopia of a small cartel where people live according to their needs and produce according to their abilities.

Dostoevsky attacks the idea of social perfection and, in particular, the idea of rational action. Social Darwinism, which was becoming extremely popular, was claiming that society could evolve and get better; to Dostoevsky, this was the ultimate absurdity. On the contrary, he felt that rational activity could never lead to betterment because man's essence transcends mere rationality:

> In a word, you can say anything about world history, everything that could come into the mind of the most disorderly imagination. Only one thing cannot be said: that it makes sense. You choke on the word. And look at what kind of thing frequently happens: you constantly meet extremely virtuous and reasonable people, great wise men and lovers of humankind whose whole purpose in life is to live

more virtuously and reasonably, that is, to shine as beacons to one's closest friends and prove to them that it is possible to live virtuously and reasonably. And then what? It's known that many of these lovers, sooner or later, even towards the ends of their lives, betray themselves, having made some sort of joke, often the dirtiest one around. Now I ask you: what can you expect from a person who is a creature endowed with such strange qualities?

Shower [a man] with all sorts of earthly blessings, drown him in happiness up to his head so that only bubbles of bliss will burst on the surface as they do in the sea; give him such economic prosperity that he'll have nothing left to do except sleep, eat cookies, and busy himself with the continuation of world history, then even this man, here, out of sheer ingratitude, out of sheer libel, will perform some kind of abominable deed [to prove] that men are still men and not the keys of a piano upon which the laws of nature play and threaten to keep playing until he wouldn't want anything more in life than a calendar. And that's not all. Even if man was only a piano key, even if you could prove this to him by the natural sciences and mathematics, even then he won't shake himself back into a reasonable state, but will, on purpose, do something

against something else, out of sheer
ingratitude, in order to have his
own way.

Unlike animals or people in socialized
society, the "free" man is always given the
tragic "choice" to make--this is the difference
between the Underground Man and the rest
of the world. Yet, as a critical realistic
writer, Dostoevsky does not endow his
Underground Man with the "perfection" that
would make theory and practice come out
evenly; on the contrary, the person writing
this work (nameless) is a liar, overly self-
conscious, vain, and "extremely intelligent."
He is a failure and, in some ways, a pitiable
creature. In this way Dostoevsky shows that
the Underground Man possesses the "fatal
element" that every human being possesses.

Through the narrator's mask, Dostoevsky
attempts to penetrate to what is real through
the distorted perceptions of the Underground
Man. This technique tries to show several
realities at once: the basic level (life as it
really is), the reality of feelings, the
"interpreted" reality of the world through the
Underground Man's rationalizations, and
finally, the reality of the Underground Man,
not as he says he is, but as he actually is.
The reader is left to judge for himself what
has actually transpired in this work.

The novel is divided into two parts. The
first is an essay, supposedly written by the
Underground Man, which examines his views
on freedom, vanity and consciousness. The
second part, entitled "Tale of the Falling
Sleet," dramatizes how the Underground Man
lives according to his principles. It quickly

becomes obvious that the Underground Man's life is guided more by feelings than by reason (note the "feeling" adjectives: loathsome, wretched, sickly, hysterical, timid, furtive, etc.). Moreover, he is ground into inaction by dwelling on every minor incident that occurs in his life; the ultimate absurdity occurs when, in a billiard parlor, he is moved out of the way by an officer who is concentrating on a good shot. For a year the Underground Man plans a revenge. Finally, he gets his chance; he bumps shoulders with the officer while passing him on a street.

The second part shows how the Underground Man attempts to assert his superiority over various individuals:

1. The Officer

2. His superior, Anton
   Antonych Setochkin

3. Simonov, a seemingly
   agreeable friend

4. Trudolyubov ("Mr. Lover-of-Work"),
   a seeker of success

5. Ferfitchikin, a follower
   of other swaggerers

6. Zverkov, ("Mr. Beastly"),
   an army officer

7. Apollon, his servant
   to whom he owes money

8. Liza, the young prostitute

With each of them, he attempts to establish a competitive relationship; and no matter what the stakes are (defined by him, not by the others), he always ends up being the humiliated one.

The potential for a relationship with Liza appears to be the strongest; but at a moment when human communication could take place, he rejects her. At the end of the work, we are left with a portrait of a man who cannot cope with life and who is doomed to remain alone.

Conclusions

Dostoevsky's ideas, his stylistic devices, his visions, his doubts, and his prejudices form an incredibly rich pastiche of ideas and pursuits presented in new, challenging ways. The 20th-century philosopher Nicholas Berdyaev looks at Dostoevsky's legacy this way:

> Dostoevsky is drunk with ideas, for in his books ideas intoxicate; but in the midst of it all, the fine edge of his intelligence is never blunted . . . all of his work is a solution of a vast problem of ideas. The hero of Notes from the Underground is an idea; Raskolnikov is an idea; Stavrogin is an idea; Kirilov, Shatov, Verkhovensky, Ivan Karamazov--ideas; all these people are, as it were, submerged by ideas, drunk with them. . . . Dostoevsky is an "idealist" writer, idealist not as that word is understood in

common speech, but in its platonic
sense.   He conceived new and
fundamental notions, but they were
always   conceived   in   motion,
dynamically.

TOLSTOY

General Background

Few writers have exerted such a tremendous influence on the world as has Count Leo Tolstoy (1828-1910). In addition to his numerous literary accomplishments such as War and Peace and Anna Karenina, Tolstoy also helped change Russian society in the 1880s and 1890s. He was the driving force behind the relocation of the persecuted Dukhobor sect, helping move them from Russia to Canada. He encouraged the Narodnik "back-to-the-people" movement, and tried to create a literature for the common man. He played an important part in the cultivation of the ethic of passive resistance and was an outspoken opponent of wars in general. His attacks on the church undermined its authority and probably helped weaken the autocratic tsarist government before the 1905 revolution. Tolstoy was an important influence on Mahatma Gandhi, George Bernard Shaw, and many others at the turn of the century.

Today, the spirit of Tolstoy's idealism is carried on through the Tolstoy Foundation. In Tolstoy's name, countless thousands of refugees have been relocated from various political tyrannies in all parts of the world. Most recently the Tolstoy Foundation has been responsible for helping numerous Soviet dissidents begin new lives in the United States.

Life

Tolstoy's life is much too long and too full of events to be recounted here in great detail. Much of his life, of course, is linked to his created works. Some of the highlights are:

1. Tolstoy was born into a well-to-do aristocratic family. Educated by foreign tutors, he was extremely well-read and intelligent. As is frequently the case with the wealthy, he had a disdain for the middle classes and a fatherly, loving feeling for the peasantry.

2. Tolstoy hardly knew his mother; she died when he was two years old. His father died when he was nine. He was brought up by other members of the family. Ironically, without an intimate experience of the day-to-day tribulations of family life, Tolstoy was to become a great moralist on how a family should be structured.

3. As a youth and then as a young adult, Tolstoy recalls having had strong sensual inclinations alternating with periods of great remorse. In 1844, at the age of sixteen, he entered the University of Kazan. He found student life dull and did not complete his studies. He then returned to his estate, Yasnaya Polyana, which for years afterwards would serve as a haven and retreat from the world.

4. Tolstoy began his writing career in 1851, when he entered the Army and went to the Caucasus to battle tribesmen. In 1854, he published Childhood, which was based

somewhat on his own experiences while he was growing up. The book was extremely successful and gave Tolstoy instant fame. From that time on, Tolstoy's writings were eagerly received in Russian journals and published almost immediately after they were submitted.

5. In 1854, Tolstoy was transferred to the Danube Front and then to Sevastopol (during the Crimean War). His Sevastopol Sketches (1855-56), about the lives and deaths of Russian soldiers, not only foreshadowed more involved descriptions of war in War and Peace, but also helped create a type of novel which depicts war from a realistic, rather than a romantic, viewpoint.

6. Most of Tolstoy's life was spent at his estate near Moscow, Yasnaya Polyana (it is now a museum and park); yet Tolstoy also experienced life in many Russian cities. In 1855 he moved to St. Petersburg, a city he did not like; and in 1857 and 1860-61, he took trips to western Europe. The "urban ways" which he experienced repulsed him, especially with regard to the effect they had on the behavior of his contemporaries; and they became objects of scorn in his novels.

7. In 1860, he witnessed the death of his brother Nicholas. This death had a profound effect on Tolstoy and is reputed to have inspired discussions of death in War and Peace, Anna Karenina, and "The Death of Ivan Ilyitch." The subject of death is one of Tolstoy's own "accursed questions" and is discussed by many of his heroes.

8. In 1862, he married Sophia Behrs. The marriage lasted the rest of his life, but

it was marred by periods of unhappiness and strife. The happy times in the marriage were recorded in the Kitty and Levin episodes of Anna Karenina. His early married years were his happiest. It was during these years that he wrote and published War and Peace (1865-69). Between 1875 and 1877 he wrote Anna Karenina.

9. While completing Anna Karenina, Tolstoy began to have doubts about the social value of his writing. A gloomy period of introspection and searching ensued, during which he did not write artistic literature (1878-85). Instead, Tolstoy began to write tracts on art and life, such as "A Criticism of Dogmatic Theology," "A Union and Translation of the Four Gospels," and "What I Believe." While few scholars doubt the sincerity of Tolstoy's searchings, many have disputed his dogmatic statements.

10. In 1886, however, Tolstoy returned to creative writing with "The Death of Ivan Ilyitch," one of his best novellas. In his later years, he alternated writing with his so-called "wanderings to the people." Some of his more famous works of this period are Resurrection (1899), and Hadji Murad (published in 1911, although written between 1896 and 1905).

11. Tolstoy had one of the most publicized deaths in Russian literary history. He died in a railroad station during one of his "wanderings" on November 7, 1910; his biographers recall that his death was witnessed not only by friends, but also by numerous newspaper reporters.

Tolstoy's Style and
the Death of Ivan Ilyitch

The "Death of Ivan Ilyitch" provides an excellent example of Tolstoy's later views fused with a good short story style.

This work presents one of Tolstoy's favorite themes: the intrusion of <u>society</u> (the world, the educated world) between an <u>individual</u> and his <u>inner self</u>. This intrusion creates a separation, and man loses his selfhood as he relates more to the rules of society than to his own self-consciousness. In this story, Tolstoy raises the question: "Is it possible for a totally social person to regain a sense of his own self?"

The opening chapter introduces a world of appearances--people who are supposedly discussing a legal case are actually reading newspapers. Mrs. Ivan Ilyitch Golovin claims to be profoundly sorrowful over the death of her husband, yet she does not show such feelings. Ivan Ilyitch's death, which might provoke a sense of grief from his co-workers, only brings out two reactions, "Who will get his position?" and "I am glad it was not I who died."

To Tolstoy, man is aware of his own selfhood only when he is aware of the world around him. In Ivan Ilyitch's world, human society has tried to shut out the world of nature, but one reality remains which cannot be ignored--<u>death</u>. From death there is no escape, and a contemplation of death makes one think about life. Pain, a purely nonrational, noncommunicable sensation, is a reminder of the natural forces at work in every person's life.

Throughout this story, society (his wife, priest, doctor) attempts to ignore the reality of death. It is only through those persons closer to nature (the peasant, Gerasim; his son) that Ivan's awareness of his own death is validated. Once he recognizes that he is indeed going to die, he can begin to reflect upon his life. Society is useless in helping Ivan confront this reality.

At the very end of the story, Ivan reviews his entire life and recognizes that he has had many failures. Once recognizing this, however, he attains a sense of peace, realizing that the past need not influence his future, and that he can always begin life anew, even when he has only a few more hours to live. Understanding this, the pain (his past), which is still there, ceases to bother him any more. Ivan Ilyitch has made a spiritual leap beyond the reality of the pain; instead of pain, there is "light" -- Tolstoy's symbol of rebirth.

THE SILVER AGE: REALISM
CHEKHOV, GORKY, KUPRIN
AND ANDREEV

By the 1890s, the Russian novel had outlived its day. New writers were concentrating on the short story and the novella (povest'). Of the many new writers, four have stood the test of time: Anton Chekhov, Maxim Gorky, Aleksandr Kuprin, and Leonid Andreev. Most writers and critics agree that Chekhov was the greatest of these--indeed, that he was one of the greatest short story writers of all time.

Chekhov

Anton Chekhov (1860-1904) stands in world literature as one of history's greatest creative artists of the short story. Using simple situations, the "slice of life" technique, Chekhov portrayed the everyday life of Russia more incisively than any other writer of his day.

It has been said that in Chekhov's world, fates of people are decided "as they have a cup of tea." This is certainly true in his major dramas: Uncle Vanya, The Seagull, Three Sisters and Cherry Orchard

Chekhov accents the loneliness of every individual. Even in his early humorous stories such as "The Orator," we discover the embarrassment of a professional orator, who, in the process of delivering a funeral oration, discovers that he is talking about the wrong man, and that the man he is describing is in the audience listening to him. In "Grief," we find the coachman Iona trying to share with his riders his grief over his son's death; when no one listens, he ends up sharing his feelings with his horse.

Of these four writers, Chekhov also had the greatest impact on world literature. Many literary critics have commented on Chekhov's "honesty" in the presentation of his characters and situations. Unlike Gorky, Kuprin and Andreev, who tend to romanticize their characters, Chekhov holds back extravagant descriptions and elaborate generalizations. Instead, he concentrates on significant moments of personal growth and change through otherwise insignificant details. His later stories, such as "Lady with a Dog," "Ward Number Six," and "House with a Mezzanine," all depict those individual experiences which give characters a degree of self-awareness and understanding which makes it impossible for them to return to a former stage in life. Chekhov's capturing of the moment of awareness is unsurpassed in Russian literature and makes him one of the greater writers of the 19th and 20th centuries.

Gorky

Maxim Gorky (1868-1936) spent his early years as a hobo. He made a striking impression on the literary world with his stories of vagabonds, gypsies, and tramps in the 1890s. His play Lower Depths created a great stir at the Moscow Art Theater in 1902, since it is one of the first plays to portray the milieu of the totally impoverished and despondent.

His early stories are forerunners of his later Autobiography, which provides a chronicle of the difficult life of poor people in the Russian empire at the turn of the century. Many of the stories tend to romanticize the plight of the poor man and sentimentalize the "goodness" of such people.

In 1921, Gorky emigrated from the USSR to Sorrento, but he returned in 1928 to assume the role of the "grand old man" of Soviet literature. He died in 1936 under mysterious circumstances.

Kuprin

Aleksandr Kuprin (1870-1938) came from a military background as well as from a life of wandering. Like Gorky, his wanderings provided him with a collection of colorful characters for his stories. In the story "Gambrinus," the hero is a saloon fiddler named Sashka who, although beaten up and maimed by detectives for trying to avoid military service, still finds a way to create music.

Kuprin's story "Anathema" features one of his most memorable characters--a large, corpulent deacon, named Olympus, who has just been told by his church to anathematize Leo Tolstoy. Olympus, however, has just been reading Tolstoy's The Cossacks; and he cannot understand how anyone who loves life with Tolstoy's intensity could be anathematized for it.

Andreev

Leonid Andreev's (1871-1919) allegorical and frequently cryptic works are intentionally shocking and morbid. Often, these stories accent the presence of the irrational, chaotic and bestial in life. His plays <u>Life of Man</u> (1905) and <u>He Who Gets Slapped</u> (1912) dramatize the dominance of Death over humanity's aspirations for love and wealth. Andreev was extremely popular in the 1920's throughout the world.

THE SILVER AGE: SYMBOLISM

During the 1890s, Russian art and literature followed separate paths. One path continued the tradition of critical realism, while the other began to explore the mystical, the ethereal, the lyrical, and the nonrealistic. This second path led to one of the great poetic schools of Russian literary history: Russian Symbolism.

Russian Symbolism first emerged in the 1890s when a group of poets began reviving what had become a dull and cliché-ridden poetry tradition. This new group centered around Valery Bryusov (1873-1924) and Dmitry Merezhkovsky (1866-1941), who searched for vivid images and new ways to express themselves. They looked back to the "golden age" of Russian poetry (the age of Pushkin and Lermontov) and to a few later romantic poets who never attained great popularity.

These poets also looked beyond the Russian borders for inspiration, particularly to the French Symbolists and German Romantics. Bryusov described the philosophy of the movement in these words:

> Art is the attaining of the world by other, not rational means. Art is what in other fields we call revelation. The creation of art is the opening of the door to eternity.

This view is reminiscent of Russian Romanticism; namely, that the poet's role in life is to uncover the irrational and the emotional and to capture it through art. The

Symbolists saw themselves as the priests of an artistic cult of beauty, which could provide the world with a new revelation of the universe.

Valery Bryusov's early poetry uses striking images and bold contrasts to present relationships between words that ordinary people might not expect:

> The rose colors are dimming
> In the pale reflection of the
>   moon.
> Tales of the sufferings of spring
> Are frozen in icebergs.
> From the outcome to the plot-
>   formation
> Dreams are wrapped in mourning
>   clothes,
> And, using the colors of silence,
> They weave garlands together.
> Under youthful daydreams' light,
> Harmonic roses do not bloom
> On the flowerbeds of discord;
> But, through the window of
>   random dreams,
> Hopes, which are put to sleep,
> Will not see the diamond stars.

Bryusov's early poems inspired others to experiment with various types of images. The resulting poetry was exciting, bold, and highly musical. Other Symbolist poets include:

1. Fyodor Sologub (1863-1927) wrote poetry which frequently depicted the demonic. His symbols fit into his own elaborate image system in which two worlds, the world of reality and the world of dreams, find themselves in conflict. In addition to poetry,

he wrote several plays and numerous prose works. His most famous novel is The Petty Demon (1905), which deals with the paranoia of a sadistic school teacher.

2. Zinaida Gippius (1867-1945) has been regarded as the feminine "double" of Sologub. While her poetry does not adhere strictly to a single image system as does Sologub's, her symbols are some of the most powerful of Russian Symbolism. Some of her more demonic works may be favorably compared to those of Edgar Allen Poe; others are more philosophical.

3. Innokenty Annensky (1856-1909), a classic scholar by vocation, fuses Symbolist themes with the rhythms of classical poetry. Many of his poems are wistful, resigned that life is not what it once was.

4. Andrei Bely (1880-1934) was known for his experimentation with images, rhythms and rhymes. In many of his experiments he attempted to bridge the gap between music and poetry. In addition, he wrote numerous prose works including St. Petersburg (1911-13), a work written on several levels.

5. Aleksandr Blok (1880-1921) is considered one of Russia's greatest poets. His poetry is much more personal than that of the other Symbolists; in many of his poems he searches for a mysterious "Unknown Lady" who represents an incarnation of a mystical "feminine" principle in the creation of the universe. His The Twelve (1918) presents a vision of the Apocalypse as part of the 1917 revolution.

TOWARD ABSTRACTION

The term "modern art," which is no longer as "modern" as it used to be, nevertheless signifies a great break in the traditions of art of the Western world. The beginnings of this break occurred throughout Europe at the turn of the century. The Russians, through their experiments in the visual arts, music, and literature, did much more than their share in bringing this new art into the light of day.

The new tendency in art was to render "abstract" or to concentrate on "form" rather than to re-create the content of a given image or experience. This tendency has been called "formalism" or, as it was called in the 1910s, "cubism." While the word "cubism" relates to a specific movement in the visual arts, it is nonetheless an excellent metaphor for the entire movement away from content-in-art: cubes are "shapes" which, while having a life of their own, also help the artist reshape reality. The artist organizes these shapes to convey his experience.

Science and technology played a significant role in creating this break in art. Scientific changes provided new means of conveying reality with much more accuracy than could be done previously. The photograph provided better reproduction of detail than did realistic painting. The motion picture could show the fluctuations and movements of everyday life with much greater accuracy than the play. Artists needed to find new ways to do things; and through their searches, they conceived new definitions of art. While theories differed, most artists agreed that one needed to concentrate on the forms and techniques of a given genre, rather than on the content. Writers looked for new ways to use words; artists looked to the textures of their paints as well as to the shapes and colors of figures; even in music, which is abstract by definition, composers experimented with the sounds made by instruments as well as with rhythms, pitches, tones, and silences.

The Visual Arts

1. The painter Isaac Levitan (1860-1900) was one of the first Russian artists to concentrate his efforts on conveying the aesthetic of the new artistic movement. Under the influence of the French Impressionists--his Twilight, Haystack (1899) is reminiscent of Monet--Levitan provided Russian art with a world of color and light in the Russian countryside. Together with Repin, Levitan is regarded by the Russians as one of their greatest painters.

If human subjects were included in a painting, then they too were presented as a reflection of light. As was true with the French Impressionists, Levitan's figures harmonized with all other shapes in the painting: the trees, sunlight reflected in the water, houses, clouds, and sky. Indeed, Levitan is considered by the Russians as their greatest landscape artist. Some of his most famous paintings reflect their subjects: Autumn Day, Sokolniki (1879), Evening Bells (1892), and Above the Eternal Calm (1894).

2. The so-called art nouveau craze of Western Europe, with its interest in graphic illustration (particularly that of Aubrey Beardsley), likewise found its supporters in turn-of-the-century Russia. In 1899, the journal Mir iskusstva (World of Art) made its appearance, published by the artist Alexander Benois, assisted by Lev Bakst and the ballet impressario, Sergei Diaghilev. This expensive journal, which survived only until 1904, reproduced many works of art. Much of its art was imitative of other styles, such as the "folkloric style" mastered by Ivan Bilibin. Bilibin's illustrations created a tradition in which Russian folk tales are illustrated. Mikhail Nesterov, whose paintings were sometimes impressionistic (Portrait of his Daughter, 1906), also used the folkloric style in some of his other paintings (In the Mountains, 1896). In the latter painting, for example, he presents a woman in peasant dress standing high over a picturesque bend in a river; the situation is much too posed to be considered "realistic" or "life-like." Nevertheless, it evokes the spirit of the Russian peasant tradition through the blending of colors in native dress with colors of the landscape.

3. Mikhail Vrubel's (1856–1910) paintings hide the realistic image to such an extent that one can hardly discover it. The female subject in Lilacs (1910), for example, appears only as a shadow within the brilliant colors of the flowers around her; the background overpowers the human subject. Like many of his contemporaries, Vrubel was fascinated by various legends and myths. His obese-yet-powerful Bogatyr (Russian Epic Hero) (1898) and Pan (1899) give new, somewhat erotic

treatments to these figures from mythology. His studies of Lermontov's Demon are perhaps his best known. In Lermontov's Demon, many of the turn-of-the-century artists saw their own plight: talented, kind, but yet damned to be perpetually misunderstood.

4. A more extreme departure from realism was made by the "Futurists," "Cubo-Futurists," and "Suprematists," whose concentration on form rather than content was combined with an attempt to shock people with the audaciousness of their art. Natalia Goncharova (1881-1962), one of Russia's first female painters, ventured into the realm of the abstract through works such as Electricity (1912), and Rayonnist Flowers (1914).

Kazimir Malevich (1878-1935) sought to "free" art from the recognizable image completely. He called this art "Suprematist" because it was free of the restrictions of three dimensions. Malevich's paintings, such as Suprematist Circle and White on White, have become famous as symbols of totally abstract art. Today, many modern abstract artists consider Malevich and Goncharova their predecessors.

Literature

1. The "Futurists" were also interested in literature, and many of them also wrote verse. As poets, they attacked bourgeois society with its interest in re-creating the beautiful. The poet-artist David Burlyuk (1882-1967), challenged all artistic traditions:

Let fate become a bitter bore
The soul a pub, the sky some
    puke.
Poetry's a worn-out whore
And beauty, a blasphemous rebuke.

2. In 1912, these poets and artists
published a manifesto, "A Slap in the Face at
Public Taste," to assail older forms of art.
Some of the poets, like Velemir Khlebnikov,
experimented with word formation and even
claimed to have created a "trans-sense"
language, which, like art, moved away from
the representational.

Incantation By Laughter
By Velemir Khlebnikov

O start laughing, laughateers!
O get laughing, laughateers!
You laughing laughs, laughify
    laughsomely!
O get laughing, superlaughsomely!
O, the belaughing minilaughing
    laugh of laughable laugha-
    teers!
O, unlaugh relaughing laughs of
    minilaughing laughateers!
    Laughation! Laughation!
Belaugh, relaugh, laughibits,
    laughibits
Laughitittles! Laughitittles!
O start laughing, laughateers!
O get laughing, laughateers!

The poet Vasily Kamensky went so far as
to abolish meaning other than what one might
derive from sounds:

Zgara-amba
Zgara-amba
Zgara-amba
Amb.
   Amb-zgara-amba
   Amb-zgara-amba
   Amb-zgara-amba
   Amb.
Shar-shor-shur-shir
Chin-drakh-tam-dzzz.

3. The Futurists' most outstanding talent
was Vladimir Mayakovsky (1893-1930). He was
destined to become the "poet laureate" of the
postrevolutionary period of New Economic
Policy in the 20s. His pre-revolutionary style
is   arrogant   and   tender,   loud   and   soft.
Mayakovsky sees himself as both the attacker
of bourgeois life and its sacrificial lamb:

   The prickly wind
   Tears out
   Furry smoke-pips
   From smokestacks black.
   The bald street lamp
   Sweetly strips
   The black stocking
   From the street's back.

The city is the sacrificer of the poet:

   Along the pavement
   Of my trampled soul
   The steps of madmen
   Stamp their cruel words.
   Where cities
   Are hung
   And in the cloud's noose
   The tired spires of towers
   Have congealed,

There I go,
Alone to moan
That crossroads
Crucify
Policemen.

After the revolution, Mayakovsky welcomed the birth of the new Soviet state, hoping that a cultural apocalypse would take place. His contribution to the culture of the 1920s will be discussed in the next chapter.

The legacy of the nonrealistic current in modern Russian creative art lives on today, despite the frowns of conservative censors and government officials. It is most frequently found in modern Russian avant-garde poetry, but it also occurs occasionally in theatrical productions and private art collections. It is perhaps most often encountered in the graphic arts, where design (i.e., form) is readily recognized as having practical merit.

Music

1. The greatest example of musical innovation in the early 20th century is the work of Igor Stravinsky (1882-1971). Stravinsky is considered one of the fathers of "modern" music of the Western world. His works include:

a. Firebird ballet (1910) composed for the ballet of Sergei Diaghilev. The score employs devices from the works of Debussy, Mussorgsky, and Rimsky-Korsakov. Nevertheless, original orchestrations are already present.

b. <u>Petrushka</u> ballet (1911) which recreates the Russian equivalent of the English "Punch and Judy" show. The music interweaves numerous folk melodies in crisp orchestrations.

c. <u>Rite of Spring</u> ballet (1913) which orchestrates a pagan Slavic religious ritual. The ballet score is full of discord and strong rhythms and almost devoid of the more traditional "melodies." When it premiered in Paris, it caused a scandal.

After World War I, Stravinsky remained in Western Europe. He died in the United States in 1971.

2. Sergei Rachmaninov (1873-1943), like Stravinsky, is regarded as an "international" composer, having spent most of his life outside his native land--much of it in Hollywood, California. To Americans, Rachmaninov's music is definitely familiar; it inspired popular songs as well as music for motion pictures. His symphonies are not performed frequently, but his piano works are popular with virtuoso pianists. His works include:

a. <u>First Symphony</u> (1897), written by the then 24-year-old composer, uses themes from a choir book of Church hymns. The influence of Tchaikowsky and Borodin is evident in this work.

b. <u>Piano Concerto #2 in C minor</u> (1900), the second of four piano concertos, is melodic in addition to requiring technical prowess from the pianist.

c. <u>Preludes</u> (1892-1902, 1903-4, 1910), are short solo pieces which contain memorable melodies and opportunities for demonstrating piano virtuosity.

NEP AND THE AGE OF
EXPERIMENTATION

The spirit of artistic experimentation pervading the prerevolutionary period did not die after 1917. The NEP (New Economic Policy) period (1921-28) was one of Russia's great artistic epochs, characterized by experimentation and debates concerning all the arts. Not all experiments were of the symbolist type; many artists worked with the devices of realism as well.

Prose

Much of the new prose dealt with the new "Red" experience of the revolution and civil war. Most of the prose was written in the traditional 19th-century realistic manner; some works, however, are highly distinctive and original, where characters and events are presented in highly unexpected ways.

1. Isaac Babel (1894-1938), like his predecessor, Anton Chekhov, was a craftsman of the short story. Babel's stories, communicating the violent world of the Civil War, are terse and frequently sensual. Stories about the Civil War, in which Babel served as a political officer, have been collected in Red Cavalry (in Russian, Horse Army). His tales of the Jewish underground in his home city are compiled as Odessa Tales (1923-24).

2. Boris Pilnyak, The Naked Year (1922). This complicated, stylized work chronicles events in the famine year of 1920. Its

symbolism is frequently obscure; its syntax, convoluted. Nevertheless, this novel influenced much writing which attempted to present the revolutionary experience in a symbolic, artistic way.

3. Dmitry Furmanov, <u>Chapayev</u> (1923). This semi-fictitious account of a guerilla leader presents the life of a partisan peasant group. At the same time, the novel affirms that even great partisan movements (and leaders) need to be harnessed and guided by the political insights of the Communist party.

4. Konstantin Fedin, <u>Cities and Years</u> (1924). This novel centers on one character, Andrei Startsov, who, as a member of the old intelligentsia finds himself without a country and, even worse, discovers that history has passed him by. While sympathetic to his plight, the novel asserts the inevitability of historical change.

5. Fyodor Gladkov, <u>Cement</u> (1925). This novel has become a classic of the Soviet reconstruction period following the Civil War. A war hero finds it difficult to adjust to the more peaceful life of a Soviet worker; as in <u>Cities and Years</u>, time is passing him by, and he must "socialize" himself to the new Soviet order. By the end of the novel, the hero has not yet accomplished his socialization.

6. Yury Olesha, whose <u>Envy</u> (1927) describes conflicts in Soviet society, and Mikhail Zoshchenko, a satirist who criticized the hypocrisy of the new elite, were both active in the pre-Stalin era. Also at this time, Mikhail Sholokhov did much of the work on his epic novel about the Don Cossacks before and after the Revolution.

7. One of the most interesting books of the NEP period is Evgeny Zamyatin's We, written in 1919-20 and published (only abroad) in 1924. We is a picture of an antiutopia; in the context of world literature, it has influenced other novels of the same type, notably, Huxley's Brave New World and Orwell's 1984.

Its author, Evgeny Zamyatin (1884-1937), considered himself a heretic and a Bohemian. Before the revolution, he participated in several revolutionary activities; but afterwards, he found himself too independent-minded to accept the various restrictions imposed by Communism. In 1931, when Zamyatin realized that he could not survive as a creative writer in the new Soviet state, he requested of Stalin himself permission to leave; and, surprisingly, it was granted. He died in Paris.

The novel posits a vision of the so-called "United State," a composite picture of the Soviet Union and Great Britain in the future. The novel is based on Zamyatin's views on the dynamics of modern industrial society. These include:

a. The forces of unity and destruction. Zamyatin saw two tendencies within society: one to unify and combine; the other to destroy and disunite. These two tendencies provide the novel's conflict.

b. The battle between science/reason and irrationality. Like Dostoevsky, Zamyatin saw governments attempting to unite by appealing to the rational and scientific. At the same time, he admired the tendency in man to be irrational and to enjoy it; the symbols for this irrationality are "the square root of minus one" and the idea of "fancy." The rulers of the United State cannot govern people's fancies away; therefore, they propose to remove them surgically.

c. To Zamyatin, heretics provide the hope for mankind. Living beyond the "Green Wall" (green probably because it is transparent and one can see the foliage through it), Zamyatin's heretics are, for the most part, artistic Bohemians who live in a loose anarchical society. Their goal for society is more to keep life enjoyable than to provide agendas and programs.

Theater

In the theater, experiments in stage production flourished. The director Vsevolod Meyerhold, one of the prime exponents of theatrical constructivist theories, created unusual stage designs which are still studied and copied today. Other directors, eager to convey the "Red" experience, attempted to render "heroic" battles and key events in the revolution. One such theatrical event was Nikolai Evreinov's Storming of the Winter Palace (1920), which was staged at the original location using as actors some of the sailors who participated in the historical event.

Poetry

In poetry, the "spirit" of this period was best expressed by Vladimir Mayakovsky (1893-1930), who had declared himself the poet "of the revolution." During the early twenties, Mayakovsky participated in virtually all of the arts: poetry, painting, and even advertising. A "Futurist" before the revolution, Mayakovsky converted his poetic style to proclaim that the future had indeed arrived. Mayakovsky's poetry screams at its readers the virtues of the revolution and of the new state. Together with the revolution, Mayakovsky advocated everything progressive, new, and industrial. He particulary liked the spirit of industry in the United States, although he tempered his enthusiasm to show that he preferred the new Soviet system.

Arts

Through the efforts of poets such as Mayakovsky and artists such as Malevich, propaganda and art were combined. Many propaganda trains and ships, equipped to educate the masses about the goals of Communism, were decorated by these famous artists.

The new style of artistic representation was particularly fitting for graphic work. The "revolutionary poster" has become an art form of its own, and posters such as D. Moor's "Have you enlisted in the volunteers" and A. Apsit's "Rise to the defense of Petrograd" have become classics in the art of posterwork.

Music

Sergei Prokofiev (1891-1953) is universally regarded as Soviet Russia's greatest composer; indeed, he will probably be regarded among the greatest Western composers of the 20th century. Unlike Stravinsky, Prokofiev could not live without his native homeland, and after a brief period of emigration he returned to the USSR. His more famous works include:

1. <u>Classical Symphony</u> (No.1) (1917), an "antiromantic" work, is written in imitation of Haydn, although it uses numerous non-classical devices. Prokofiev is said to have written this piece without the aid of a musical instrument. As in most of his works, Prokofiev uses musical humor in many passages.

2. <u>Love for Three Oranges</u> (1921) is a comic opera, written in the United States and performed for the first time in Chicago. Spoofing both opera and the fairy tale, this work is extremely popular in the Soviet Union. Its "March" has become famous as a separate orchestral piece.

3. <u>Lieutenant Kizhe</u> (1934) is one of Prokofiev's scores for the cinema. It has been reorchestrated as a suite.

4. <u>Peter and the Wolf</u> (1936), a musical novelty popular in the United States, combines narration with an introduction to instruments in the orchestra.

5. <u>Fifth Symphony</u> (1944), a brilliantly orchestrated antiromantic work, throbbing

with pulsating rhythms, highly original melodies, and discordant harmonies.

Cinema

Many film historians claim that Soviet films of the 1920s influenced today's cinema. The films produced at this time, which chronicled the revolution and the first years of reconstruction, have also become classics of the propaganda art form. These include:

1. Sergei Eisenstein's Potemkin (1925), Strike (1925), Alexander Nevsky (1938), Ivan the Terrible (1930s-'40s).

2. Lev Kuleshov's The Incredible Adventures of Mister West in the Land of the Bolsheviks (1924).

3. Vsevolod Pudovkin's Mother (1926), The End of St. Petersburg (1927).

4. Alexander Dovzhenko's Zvenigora (1927), Arsenal (1929), Earth (1930).

However, while the arts expressed a hope for a new order, the bureaucrats and administrators who were the scourge of the Russian intelligentsia in the 19th century returned wearing Soviet uniforms. By the end of the 1920s, many poets and artists either stopped working or emigrated to the West.

SOCIALIST REALISM

The Silver Age and NEP periods saw a division in art between the "representational" and the "abstract." Art which was representational provided a much better means to communicate social messages and comments on society. Thus, Soviet propagandists endorsed the use of representational or "realistic" art to advocate the Communist system. Abstract art was condemned for being "formal" and not progressive in promoting the goals of Communism.

The 1930s

1. As Josef Stalin was consolidating his power, official criticism mounted against the so-called "formalism" of the experimenting artist. The official party line proclaimed that writing was to be clear and contain a social message. Lenin, after all, felt that art was a powerful means to carry the message of the state to the people; the more accessible the art, the more carefully it must be watched by ideologues. By the mid-thirties, literature and the fine arts were totally under the control of the state. The only nonpolitical art tolerated was realistic portraiture and still-life painting. For the most part, literature and the fine arts were harnessed to sing accolades to the industrial hopes and achievements of the Stalinist state.

2. In 1934, the Organizational Committee of the Soviet Writers' Union defined the term to describe this art; it was called "Socialist Realism":

Socialist Realism, being the basic method of Soviet imaginative literature and literary criticism, demands from the artist a truthful, historically accurate depiction of reality in its revolutionary development. At the same time, this truthfulness and historical accuracy of the artistic depiction of reality must be combined with the task of the ideological molding and education of the working people in the spirit of socialism. (Ustav Soyuza sovetskikh pisatelei, Pravda, Literaturnaya gazeta, May 6, 1934.)

3. Art was to serve as an expression of the collective, of the masses rather than of the individual. Art had to contain three ideas: partynost', ideynost', and narodnost'.

a. Partynost' ("party-ness"): art must become a part of the general proletarian cause as expressed first by the Communist Party.

b. Ideynost' ("idea-ness"): art must have an influence over the viewer; there must be a socialist content based on Marxist-Leninist aesthetics.

c. Narodnost' ("people-ness"): the work must relate to the spirit of the working masses.

4. These aesthetic requirements are very difficult to attain, since they are invariably judged after the fact--that is, after the work is created. Art, according to Socialist Realist doctrine, must appear bold;

yet it is interpreted and judged by persons who know little about aesthetics. The result has become an especially timid art, which relies heavily on tried and long-used artistic conventions of the 19th century. In addition, the topics chosen have been mostly dull, such as the collectivization of a farm, or "safe," such as the Civil War (where the Reds always triumph) or Lenin.

5. Nevertheless, one occasionally encounters a comment about the anxieties of the present disguised in a painting or work of literature. In Petrov-Vodkin's 1934 painting Alarm, a man is shown looking out of his window while his family stands nearby, visibly frightened. Ostensibly, the situation depicts Civil War strife in 1919 when Reds and Whites were battling each other in city streets. Yet, the situation could depict Soviet life in 1934, when the Secret Police were taking innocent people away in the middle of the night for alleged crimes and no one knew who would be next.

6. Even in the domain of music—which basically transcends the representational—one discovers the specter of art by governmental decree. Dmitry Shostakovich (1906-75) is considered by many to be as good as Prokofiev. Like Prokofiev, Shostakovich's early works were antiromantic with form taking precedence over melody. In 1934, however, he came under attack; his music was reputed to be "negative." In order to recant, he wrote his Fifth Symphony, in which he abandoned the grotesque and the "formal" for more tuneful music in the tradition of the 19th century, with only occasional meek flares of discord. In 1937, this symphony was

praised in Pravda. In more recent times, Shostakovich has written both traditional and nontraditional music. Some of it is intensely patriotic, such as his Leningrad Symphony (7th Symphony, 1942) and his more recent Babi Yar Symphony (13th Symphony, 1962), which commemorates the slaughter of Jews by the Nazis in Kiev during World War II.

7. The literature of the period (1928-39) is characterized by a number of so-called "tractor" novels, some of which still possess literary merit. V. P. Katayev's Time, Forward and Leonid Leonov's The Thief have been singled out by many literary critics as possessing good plots and interesting characterizations. The autobiographical How the Steel was Tempered by Nikolai Ostrovsky depicts a writer who, although he is losing his eyesight, can still inspire others by his enthusiasm for socialism. Y. Krymov's Tanker Derbent has not fared as well. Its plot concerns the turning of diesel screws in an oil tanker and the attempts made by the crew to make them turn faster.

Today, "Socialist Realism" is still the official style of art in the USSR. Since Stalin's death, however, the term is given more lip service than in the 1930s. The most obvious examples of Socialist Realist art remain the monuments and memorials built by the state to commemorate the achievements of Socialism and the battles of World War II.

AFTER STALIN

The Thaw

It is always difficult to discuss current trends and notable figures of a nation's literature, music, and art. For the most part, these trends do not stand the test of time--the buffer zone for literary and art critics--and evaluation often amounts to guesswork.

Since 1956, Soviet writers and artists have been freer than during the days of Stalin:

1. Since Stalin's death, literature and art have been moving away from the "we" of the tractor novel and focusing more on the "I" of personal experience.

2. Socialist Realism still remains the official party line and is thus expounded in all publications, yet more non-Socialist Realist works (without much emphasis on a social message) are emerging in print.

3. An "underground" literature has emerged which is critical of the state. For the most part, this is called Samizdat (self-publishing), with a corollary movement called Magnitizdat on tape.

The new trend has usually been referred to as "The Thaw"--although there have been both freezes and thaws in the relationship between the government and the artist during the last 25 years. The title of this new movement is taken from a novel by Ilya

Ehrenburg (1954) in which the hero is an artist who paints for himself rather than for the state.

Pasternak and Doctor Zhivago

The most notorious instance of the political repression of literature during the 1950s was the novel Doctor Zhivago, written by Boris Pasternak and published in the United States (in translation) in 1958. Pasternak is considered one of the major figures in Russian poetry of the 20th century. A product of the Silver Age, he began writing in the 1920s. He experienced political difficulties during the height of the Stalinist repressions; and rather than sell out to Socialist Realism, he ventured into translation. Today he is considered Russia's foremost translator of Shakespeare.

His Doctor Zhivago is a labor of love and a masterpiece of poetic prose. It is difficult to classify as a novel because of its long poetic passages, coincidences in the plot, and philosophical discourses. Nevertheless, it chronicles Russian history at some of its most difficult moments and, at the same time, makes a powerful pacifist statement.

Pasternak was a victim of Khrushchev's ignorance. His purge was unnecessary as he did not threaten the state, and most Soviets agree that Doctor Zhivago is not patently anti-Soviet. His grave in Peredelkino (near Moscow) is visited daily by persons interested in the arts, and it has become a shrine for the cause of freedom in Soviet letters.

Solzhenitsyn

The literature of dissidence and criticism of the state is centered around the figure of Aleksandr Solzhenitsyn, who has been forcibly exiled by the Soviet government. A one-time victim of Stalin's purges, his One Day In the Life of Ivan Denisovich (1962) chronicles the sober reality of the labor camps of the 1940s, a subject that every Soviet citizen knows well. His later novels, all of which deal with the moral and ethical questions pertaining to the purges, were not published in the USSR (unlike One Day, which was). These works include Cancer Ward and The First Circle. In his Gulag Archipelago series, he attempts to write Soviet history "the way it actually happened," contending that most Soviets know little about their own history since it is constantly being rewritten to please Soviet leaders.

Poetry

After the death of Stalin, a new, more personal kind of poetry became popular. It was through poetry that personal experiences could best be expressed and communicated orally. The so-called "new" poets Andrei Voznesensky, Bella Akhmadulina and Evgeny Evtushenko were especially popular. All three (as well as others) have occasionally fallen into disfavor with the state, but have managed to continue writing and publishing poetry.

Andrei Voznesensky's style is brash and direct, with touches of humor. In his poems one discovers both universal experience and the stance of the lonely creative poet.

Bella Akhmadulina, the most brilliant female voice of this group, tends to be whimsical but also personal.

Evgeny Evtushenko's name is the best-known of these poets; he has frequently toured the West. Playing a careful game of political tight-rope walking, he has survived bitter criticism from the authorities while at the same time managing to write social criticism. His "Babi Yar" poem discusses the murder of Jews by the Nazis in Kiev. "Stalin's Heirs" is a brave presentation of the premise that some persons in Soviet government would like to return to the repressions of Stalin. Evtushenko criticizes persons who try to escape from responsibility to their society.

APPENDIX I
SOVIET SPORTS

General

1. Soviet sports are highly regarded around the world. No other nation in recent history has won more Olympic medals and world championships than the USSR.

2. Soviet sports and good physical conditioning are strongly emphasized throughout the USSR. The Soviets claim that, in 1978, over 55 million Soviet citizens regularly participated in some form of sports activity (e.g., they belong to sports clubs).

3. Soviet sports activities are organized at all levels. These include:

a. Compulsory physical education in all schools at least twice a week.

b. Sports clubs, under the administration of local schools, where students may practice and play after hours.

c. Sports schools operating after school hours for children with special athletic potential. Over two million children attended these schools in 1978.

d. Sport-oriented forms and schools, where one or more sports are part of the curriculum of the school.

e. Sports clubs at factories, collective farms, and colleges for sports-minded adults. Over 220,000 of these clubs exist Union-wide.

f. Voluntary Sports Societies, which unite sports clubs into national competitions. These are organized for the most part by trade.

g. The Sports Committee of the USSR, a government agency, which promotes and administers Soviet policy towards physical culture. It provides guidance and recommendations to the Voluntary Sports Societies but does not regulate them.

h. The USSR Olympic Committee, which promotes international competition, ranging from good-will tours to the Olympic Games.

Sports Facilities

The Soviets are proud of their many sports facilities, ranging from school gymnasiums to massive sports complexes. In their 1980 pamphlet, Sport (Novosti Press Agency), the following statistics were provided regarding major sports installations:

Gyms	63,423
Skiing centers	5,998
Stadiums	3,200
Swimming pools	1,344

Western observers, however, have noted that the most advanced facilities are primarily available to the national and international contenders, and not to the amateurs.

Sports in Everyday Life

1. Sports are emphasized in much Soviet official writing and propaganda. The new Soviet Constitution of 1977 states that the government "encourages the development of mass physical culture and sports." Good physical conditioning encourages a physical readiness in the event of war and promotes good health in Soviet factories, collective farms, and universities.

2. "Physical culture breaks" of five minutes apiece are provided in Soviet factories and offices. Specified exercises are recommended to encourage workers to get rid of fatigue and keep alert. These are called "five minutes of vim and vigor."

3. A "Sportloto" program, with the motto "You Win--Sports Win," is conducted nationally. People buy lottery tickets to promote sports. A winner may win up to half the sale of lottery tickets; the other half goes toward the building of sports facilities.

4. An all-Union sports competition is designed to encourage all people to participate in a sport, at least on the local level. These local competitions lead to the Spartakiads, in which athletes are selected for the Olympics. In the 1979 Spartakiad, the USSR opened the doors for non-Soviets to participate as well.

5. The USSR awards various medals for physical fitness. On the local level, first- and second-class badges are awarded to all persons who meet the requirements set for various events. These requirements differ

according to age group. Beyond these
medals, champion athletes are awarded
ratings medals (first, second and third) and,
on a higher level, the Candidate Master of
Sport, the USSR Master of Sport, and the
USSR Master of Sport International Class.
The highest medal is the Merited Master of
Sport of the USSR, which is an honorary title
given to record-holders and to Olympic
champions.

Status of an Athlete

1. Since sport is regarded as a means of
promoting good health at home and, at the
same time, propagandizing the USSR abroad,
champion athletes in the Soviet Union receive
preferential treatment.

2. Athletes frequently receive better
apartments, private coaching, trips abroad,
and other benefits for their work for the
government.

3. Frequently, athletes are used as
"good-will ambassadors" to promote good
feelings toward the USSR.

Sport As a Science

1. The USSR regards sport as a science
and has made numerous studies regarding the
human body, its relationship to the mind, and
the various physical and mental requirements
needed to excel in a given sport. Currently
there are 300,000 specialists in physical
culture in the USSR; they are trained at 24
state physical culture institutes as well as in

various departments in colleges and pedagogical schools.

2. Potential athletes are identified early --on the basis of their physical features, their agility, etc.--and encouraged to participate in a given sport. Those who live up to their potential may attend one of the special sports schools, where they will practice only one sport.

3. The Soviets are developing a field of "Sports Medicine," which is designed to sustain sports prowess in athletes, maintain stamina, and avoid sports injuries. Research in sports fields is currently being conducted in Sports Institutes in Moscow, Leningrad, Kiev, and Tbilisi.

Soviet Olympic Medal Achievements

1952	71
1956	114
1960	124
1964	121
1968	104
1972	115
1976	152
1980	196

(The source for this section is Catherine O'Brien, who is thanked for her contribution.)

APPENDIX II
PASSAGES FROM LITERARY WORKS
DISCUSSED IN THE <u>OUTLINE</u>

PUSHKIN
    Epigrams and Poems
    "The Poet"
    from "Tatyana's Dream" in
    <u>Eugene Onegin</u>

LERMONTOV
    "The Angel"

GORKY
    from "A Man is Born"
    "Konovalov"

KUPRIN
    from "Gambrinus"
    from "Anathema"

CHEKHOV
    from "Grief"

SOLOGUB
    "The Devil's Swing"

GIPPIUS
    "The Spiders"
    "Nonlove"

BELY
    from "Glosalolia"
    "In the Hills"

BLOK
    "I Sense Your Closeness"

BABEL
    "Cemetery at Kozin"

MAYAKOVSKY
    "Brodvei" ("Broadway")

VOZNESENSKY
    "I'm Goya"
    "Parabolic Ballad"

EVTUSHENKO
    "The Beatnik Girl"

AKHMADULINA
    "The New Blast Furnace in the Kemerovo
        Metallurgical Combine"

PUSHKIN

Epigrams and Poems

The Story of a Versifier

At first, espying with his ear
    A sound,
Then writing with his passion dear
    A mound
He tortures us with all his noisy
    Tricks
Then prints it--splash--into the
    Styx!

Epigram on A. Davydova

One man slept with our Aglaya,
With uniform and black mustache,
A Frenchman found her soul on fire,
A yet one more! 'cause he had cash.
Cleon, because his mind was higher,
Damis, because he sang so well.
So now, my dearest friend Aglaya,
What is your husband for, pray tell?

On Count Vorontsov

Semi-milord and semi-bore,
Semi-wise and semi-dope,
Semi-crook, but there is hope,
He'll be a full one on this score.

To the Emperor,
Nicholas I

No sooner was he tsar,
When miracles were done.
A hundred twenty were sent far
Into Siberia. And five were hung.

The Poet

Before that time when God Apollo
Calls the poet to his task,
The poet will not want to follow,
Of noble deeds, he's loathe to ask.
His lyre's abandoned on the earth;
His soul is sleeping, frozen-chilled.
Of children with just normal birth,
He is perhaps the weakest willed.
But once he hears the godly verb,
And feels it in his inner ear,
The poet's soul becomes disturbed,
As eagle's feathers stirred in fear,
He gets perturbed while watching
    pleasure,
He moves away from human speech.
To nation's idols of great treasure
He does not speak, nor e'en beseech.
He runs amuck, all wild and homely,
With irritating sounds he bounds and
    flees.
To shores of oceans cold and lonely,
To forests whispering with
    trees. . . .

From "Tatyana's Dream"
in <u>Eugene Onegin</u>

As to a bitter separation
Tatyana ambles up the stream,
And yet, there's no relation
To help her cross it, in this dream.

But then, a hummock starts to rustle,
What ugly creature starts to bustle?
A big dishevelled ugly bear,
Tatyana, oh!   And from his lair,
He roars out, baring crooked claws.
He goes for her and she all tense,
With trembling hands gropes for
    defense
And frightened, she steps back and
    draws
Across the stream, all safe.   Untrue.
The bear still comes, what can she do?

LERMONTOV

The Angel

In heaven, at night, an angel did fly
    and quietly sang his song in the
    sky.
The moon and the stars and the clouds
    in a throng
Listened at once to this heavenly
    song.

He sang of the bliss of souls without
    sin,
Who live in the gardens of Heaven
    within.
Of God Almighty he sang, and his
    praise
Will last to the very end of all
    days.

A young soul he took o'er the
    heavenly spheres,
To the world of sadness and tears.
And the sound of his song remained in
    the soul
Without words--but beautifully whole.

And long on the earth, the soul lan-
    guished alone
Full of hope for the heavenly home.
And the songs of the heavens remained
    of more dearth
Than the flaccid dull songs of the
    earth.

GORKY

From "A Man Is Born"

A quiet moan in the bushes, a human moan which always rouses the soul in kinship.

Pushing the bushes aside, I saw--with her back propped up against the walnut tree--a peasant woman sitting, wearing a yellow kerchief, her head lowered on her shoulder, her mouth freakishly distended, her eyes bulging and senseless. She was holding her hands on her enormous belly and was breathing so frighteningly unnaturally that her entire stomach heaved convulsively; and the woman, pressing at it with her hands, was mooing softly and baring her yellow, wolf-like teeth.

"What happened, did they hit you?" I asked, bending over her. She moved her bare legs back and forth in the ashen dust like a fly; and bobbing her heavy head up, she rasps, "Go away-y-y, shameless man, go away-y-y."

I understood what this was all about. I had already seen this once. Of course, I got scared and jumped back; and the woman let out a loud, long-drawn howl. From her eyes, which were ready to burst, gushed some cloudy tears, which then flowed down her purplish and tightly blown-up face.

This brought me back to her. I threw my knapsack, kettle, and pot onto the ground and tried to bend her legs at the knees. She pushed me aside, hitting my face and chest with her hands; and, turning on me like a she-bear, she growled and rasped and finally went into the bushes on all fours.

"Robber, devil. . . "

Her arms gave way; she fell, poked her face into the ground and began to howl all over again, convulsively stretching her legs.

In the fever of the excitement, I quickly remembered everything that I ever learned about such things and overturned her onto her back and bent her legs. The chorion had already been dropped down.

"Stay down, you'll be giving birth soon."

I ran to the sea, rolled up my sleeves, washed my hands, came back, and became a male midwife.

The woman writhed, like birch-bark in a flame. She patted the ground around her with her hands; and pulling out the withered grass, she tried to stuff it into her mouth. She spattered soil on her strange inhuman face with its wild, bloodshot eyes. The chorion, by now, had burst and a little head was peering through. I had to hold the convulsions down and help the child, being careful that she did not stuff the grass into her twisted, moaning mouth. We cursed at each other quietly, she through her teeth and I, too, quietly--she from pain and probably from shame, while I from embarrassment and tormented pity for her.

"Oh God," she rasped, her blue lips bitten through and foamy; and her eyes, as if they were bleached by the sun, were still streaming with the abundant tears of the unbearable suffering of a mother. Her entire body was breaking in two.

"Go away, you devil."

She continued to push me away with her weak, strained arms while I was saying, convincingly,

"You simple fool, give birth, come on, faster."

I'm tormented with pity for her, and I feel that her tears have gushed into my eyes; my heart is constrained with grief; I want to scream and do scream, "Come on, hurry up!"

And suddenly, there's a man in my arms. All red. Even through my tears, I see him: he's all red and is already dissatisfied with the world. He's wiggling and screaming at the top of his lungs, even though he's still tied to his mother. His eyes are blue, his nose is pressed down in a funny way into his red squashed face. His lips move and intone, "Ya-a-a, ya-a-a. . . ."

A new inhabitant of the Russian land, a person of unknown destiny, was cradled in my arms, solidly snorting. The sea splashed and slushed, all in white lacy currents. The bushes shushed, the sun shone; it was now past midday.

We walked quietly; sometimes the mother would stop, sigh deeply, or toss her head up, looking to all sides--to the sea, the woods and the mountains--and then she would peer into her son's face. His eyes, washed through and through by the tears of suffering, were again incredibly clear, again flowering and burning with the blue flame of inexhaustible love.

Then she stopped and said, "oh my Lord, my God! It's so good, so good!"

And that was it. She would have walked and walked to the ends of the earth; and he, her little son, would have grown, grown in the freedom of the open world, close to his mother's breast, my birth-giving one.

Loud sounds the sea, sounds the sea.

From "Konovalov"

"How about the one on Stenka Razin?"
"About Stenka? Fine!"
"Very well."
"Go ahead."

And soon I was reading him Kostomarov's "The Rise of Stenka Razin." At first the talented almost-epic-poem monologue didn't appeal to my bearded listener.

"Just how come there aren't any conversations here?" he asked, looking into the book. And when I explained why, he simply yawned and tried to hide it. When this didn't work, he got flustered and proclaimed guiltily, "Read on, it's all right! This is just how . . . ."

While the historian was painting the figure of Stepan Timofeevich with his artist's brush and the "Prince of the Volga Volunteers" was emerging from the book's pages, Konovalov was reborn. At first he was bored and indifferent, his eyes clouded with lazy dreaminess. Later, gradually and imperceptibly, he began to behave in a completely new way. Sitting on the bin opposite me and hugging his knees, he placed his chin on them in such a way that his beard covered his legs. He looked at me with hungry, strangely burning eyes from under sternly furled brows.

You would think that Konovalov, not Frolka, was Razin's blood brother. There appeared to be some sort of enduring blood tie which had existed for three centuries and which, to this day, bound this hobo to Stenka. This hobo, with all the vigor of his vibrant, strong body, with all the passion of his soul pining away, could feel the pain and wrath of the free falcon captured some three hundred years ago.

"Read on, for Christ's sake . . . ."

I read, excited and worried, feeling my heart beat, and, together with Konovalov, experienced Stenka's grief. And then we came upon the tortures.

Konovalov gnashed his teeth; his blue eyes glittered like coals. He leaned over me and kept his eyes glued to the book. I shook my head to get him away from me. Konovalov noticed this and placed the entire weight of his heavy palm on my head.

"Then Razin gnashed his teeth so hard that he spat some out with blood."

"Enough, damn it!" cried Konovalov. Tearing the book out of my hands, he smacked it against the floor with all his might and then lowered himself over it.

He was crying, and since he was ashamed of his tears, he growled in a funny way so he wouldn't sob. He hid his face in his lap and cried, wiping his eyes on his dirty twilled trousers.

I sat in front of him on the bin not knowing how to console him.

"Maxim," Konovalov said, sitting on the floor. "It's scary! Pila, Sysoika. And then Stenka, hey? What a fate! And he spat his teeth out, hey?"

His body was shuddering. He was especially amazed by Stenka's spat-out teeth. He kept on talking about them while feverishly twitching his shoulders.

We were both like drunkards under the influence of the cruel and torment-laden picture of the tortures which had arisen before us.

"Read it to me again, you hear?!" Konovalov entreated me, having pushed the book up and handed it to me. "And now show me where the business about the teeth is written."

I showed him, and his eyes locked on the passage. "And it's written here, 'he spat his teeth out with blood?' But the letters are the same as all the others. Oh, God! How it must have hurt, hey? Even his teeth.

And in the end, what else is there? The execution? A-ha! Glory be to God, they'll execute the man all the same!"

He expressed this joy with such zeal and delight in his eyes that I shuddered at this compassion which wanted so strongly the death of the tortured Stenka.

The whole day passed in a strange fog. We talked about Stenka all the time, recalling his life, the songs written about him, his tortures. A couple of times, Konovalov would break into song in his clear baritone voice and then break it off.

From that day forward, he and I became even closer.

KUPRIN

From "Gambrinus"

Now for the second and final time, Sashka was considered dead and buried. Someone saw the entire scene that took place on the sidewalk by the beer hall and told the others about it. Experienced people who sat at Gambrinus's who knew what kind of an establishment the Boulevard station house was and what kind of a thing the revenge of detectives was.

But now the people worried a lot less about Sashka's fate than they had the first time and forgot him a lot quicker. In two months, a new fiddler (Sashka's student), found by the accompanist, sat in his place. And then, one quiet spring day about three months later, when the musicians were playing the "Anticipation" waltz, someone's frail voice cried in a fright, "Hey lads, it's Sashka!"

Everybody turned around and moved away from the kegs. Yes, it was the twice-resurrected Sashka all right, now bearded, emaciated and pale. The people ran over to him, surrounding him, shoving and poking him while giving him mugs of beer. Then suddenly the same voice yelled, "Brothers, his arm, look at it!"

Everyone suddenly got still. Sashka's left arm, gnarled and literally smashed, was twisted with the elbow to his side. It didn't seem either to bend or unbend, and his fingers were sticking out permanently toward his chin.

"What happened, comrade?" the hairy boatswain from the "Russian Society" finally asked.

"Forget it. . .it's some tendon or other," answered Sashka calmly.

"Well. . ."

Again, everyone was silent.

"Does this mean the end of the 'Chaban'?" asked the boatswain sympathetically.

"The 'Chaban'?" echoed Sashka, and his eyes began to play. "Hey you!" he ordered the accompanist with his usual self-confidence, "The 'Chaban'! Ein, zwei, drei!"

The pianist took off playing a gay dance, looking back with mistrust. But with his good hand, Sashka pulled out of his pocket some kind of small, palm-sized, long, black instrument with a stem and stuck the stem into his mouth. Then, bending his whole body to the left to the extent that his maimed, motionless arm would let him, he suddenly began to toot the deafeningly gay "Chaban" on the ocarina.

"Ho-ho-ho," resounded the joyous laughter of the audience.

"Well, damn!" exclaimed the boatswain and then, suddenly even for him, made a clever dance entrance and began moving his knees back and forth. Caught up by this move, the guests also began to dance, women and men alike. Even the waiters, trying not to lose their composure, smilingly shuffled their feet from place to place.

Madame Ivanova, having forgotten that she was the captain on watch, nodded her head to the beat of the fiery dance and lightly snapped her fingers. And, perhaps, even the old Gambrinus, full of holes from time, moved his eyebrows, gaily looking out onto the street. It seemed that out of the maimed, emaciated Sashka, the pitiful, simple whistle sang in a language unfortunately not yet understood by either Gambrinus' friends or Sashka himself.

"That's all right! Man may be crippled, but art will prevail and conquer everything!"

From "Anathema"

. . . [Olympus] didn't hear it, but he guessed at the weak mumblings of the old priest.

"May the Lord God bless our proto-deaconry. May he anathematize the blasphemer and apostate from the faith of Christ who whorishly rejected the sweet mysteries of God, Count Leo Tolstoy. In the name of the Father, Son and Holy Ghost."

And suddenly, Olympus felt that the hairs of his head were pointing in various directions and that they were becoming heavy and hard, like steel wire. And at the same moment, the wonderful words of yesterday's story floated up with incredible clarity:

. . . he lifted his head and began to stare intently at the

moths, which were fluttering over the wavering candle flame and falling into it.

"Oh, you stupid thing," he said, "where are you flying? Stupid! Stupid!" He raised himself and with his thick fingers began to shoo away the moths.

"You'll burn up, stupid thing; here, fly here, there's a lot more room," he added gently, trying to catch it carefully by its wings and let it go free. "You're doing yourself in, and I pity you."

"Oh my God, whom am I cursing?" thought the deacon in horror. "Not him? Why, I cried all night from joy, from being touched, from tenderness."

But, faithful to the thousand-year-old habit, he let drop the horrible shattering words of the curse; and they fell into the crowd like the peals of an enormous brass bell.

". . . The former priest Nikita and monks Sergius, Sabbatius, and even Sabbatius Dorotheus and Gabriel blaspheme the church's mysteries and do not want to repent and submit to the true church. For these deeds, repellent to God, may they be accursed."

The protodeacon suddenly stopped and shut the ancient prayerbook with a thump. In it were even more horrible curses--curses which, when compared to the confessions of regular people, could only have been concocted by the narrow minds of monks in the first centuries of Christianity.

His face turned blue, almost black. His fingers clutched convulsively at the pulpit's rail. For a moment he thought he would faint, but he straightened himself up; and, harnessing his powerful voice to the fullest, he began ceremoniously:

"To our earthly joy, the ornament and flower of life, truly the servant and comrade-at-arms of Christ, Count Leo. . . ."

He was silent for a second. And at this time in the jam-packed church, you could not hear a cough or a whisper or a shuffle. It was that horrid moment of quiet when a crowd of many hundreds is silent, submitting itself to a single will, overcome by one feeling. And now, the protodeacon's eyes filled with tears and immediately turned red. For a moment, his face became beautiful, as beautiful as a man's face can become in a moment of inspiration. He cleared his throat once more and mentally tried to lower his voice by two half-tones; suddenly, filling the enormous cathedral with his supernatural voice, he wailed out:

"Long l-i-i-i-fe."

And instead of following the rite of anathematization by lowering the candle, he raised it high into the air.

Vainly the choirmaster hissed at his urchins, thumping several on their heads with his tuning fork and shutting their mouths with his hand. Joyfully, like the silver sounds of the archangels' trumpets, their screams filled the entire church, "Long, long, long life."

Into the pulpit climbed the father superior, the father provost, the consistory clerk, the psalm reader and the excited wife of the deacon.

"Leave me, leave me in peace," said the father Olympus in an angry, whistling whisper and scornfully pushed the father provost aside with his hand. "I've strained my voice, but it was to God's glory and to his . . . move away!" Behind the altar, he removed his brocaded vestments, kissed the stole in farewell with great tenderness, blessed himself before the altar image and walked down into the cathedral. He walked a whole head higher than the people--big, majestic, and melancholy--and the people stepped aside, involuntarily and with a strange fear, forming a wide path. Stonily he walked by the bishop's throne, not even glancing in that direction and came out onto the porch.

It was in the cathedral square that the little wife first caught up with him; and, weeping and pulling him by his cassock's sleeve, she began to prattle:

"What did you do, you damn fool! You've downed too much vodka from the morning, you filthy drunk. You'll be lucky if you're only sent away to a monastery to clean outhouses, you lumbering oaf. How many people do I have to make up with now because of you, you Herod! Stupid wretch, you've ruined my life!"

"It makes no difference," the deacon hissed, looking at the ground. "I'll go load bricks, I'll become a switchman, a streetsweeper; but I'll have to remove my habit anyway. Tomorrow, I don't want to remain. I don't wish to. My soul can't stand it. I truly believe in Christ and the Apostolic Church according to the symbol of the faith, but I won't suffer malice. God has given everything for man's joy," he suddenly stated the familiar words.

"You fool, oaf," screamed the wife. "You say, for joy! I'll go to the governor, to the Tsar himself. You've drunk yourself into delirium, you big log."

The father Olympus stopped, turned to her and, opening his big, angry bovine eyes, said heavily and soberly, "Well?"

And for the first time in her life, his wife shut up, walked away from her husband, covered her nose with her handkerchief and began to cry.

And he walked on, immeasurably enormous, black and majestic, like a monument.

CHEKHOV

From "Grief"

"Are you chewing?" Iona asks his horse, seeing its glowing eyes. "Well then, chew away, chew away; if we haven't ridden around enough for oats, then we'll eat hay. Yes, I'm getting too old to drive. My son should drive, not I. He was a real cabby. If only he were alive."

Iona is quiet for a moment, and then he continues, "Well, brother, that's how it was, dear mare of mine. Kuzma Ionich is gone. Departed from life. Up and died for no reason at all. Now look, let's say you have a little colt and you're this colt's own mother. And suddenly, let's say, this same colt departs from life. It's sad, isn't it?"

The horse keeps chewing while listening and breathing on her master's hands.

Iona forgets all else and tells her everything.

SOLOGUB

The Devil's Swing

Above the water's ring
Where shaggy pine trees stand,
The devil rocks his swing
With his hairy hand.

He swings it ever mocking
    Forth and back,
    Forth and back,
The plank is creaking, rocking,
Against the bark it's knocking,
This ever-tightening strand.

Its whine is never-ending
This plank, it really rides,
And the devil's laughing, bending
As he's grabbing both his sides.

I'm grasping, reaching, swinging,
    Forth and back,
    Forth and back,
I'm grasping and I'm clinging,
And trying to get winging,
From his hungry glance.

Above the pine trees winging,
Screeches a blue one in the sky,
"All right, so now you're swinging,"
"So devil take you, fly!"

Where shadows dusk are bringing
Others squeal and cry,
"All right, so now you're swinging,"
"So devil take you, fly!"

This plank on which I ride
He'll keep rocking, this I know,
Until he'll smash my hide
With a mighty blow.

But not before the rope hemp
Will get rubbed in twain.
Not before the earth-damp
Will rise up again.

I'll soar up past the treetop
Then smash the earth below
Swing on, you devil, don't stop
Swing higher, higher . . . oh!

GIPPIUS

Spiders

I'm in a cell without a door,
The cell is tight and low;
In each of its four corners, four
Ugly spiders show.

They're filthy, fat and agile,
And they weave and weave and weave.
And their fearsome and unfragile
Work they never, never leave.

Four smaller webs have now grown
And are now one in this must,
Their backs are fully shown
In the dim and evil dust.

The webs my eyelids touch;
They're sticky-grey and soft.
And their delight is much,
These four beasts aloft.

Nonlove

You pound the shutters like wet wind
    blowing,
Like blackest wind you sing, "You're
    mine."
"I'm Ancient Chaos, I'm here showing
You the way; open up, resign!"

I hold them fast. I do not bring
Myself. I hide my fear,
I hold and hope, I hold, I cling
To one last ray, my love so dear.

Blind Chaos laughs, it says only,
"You'll die in chains, release your
        fetter,
You know what's happy, you're still
        lonely,
There's joy in freedom, nonlove is
        better!"

Becoming chill, a prayer I prattle,
My prayer to love is weakly done.
My arms grow weak, I cease the
        battle,
The door is open, you have won!

BELY

From "Glossalolia"

How did the world of consonants come into being? It was thrown into nothingness--into the cavity of the mouth-exhaling heat; and sounds came together around the circle of the larynx: the heats carried themselves forward in an ever-widening stream up to the exit of the throat. In the flying noiselessness stood the lightest--"h". . . . The noise of exhaling heat is the Beginning. In the Beginning is the heat, and the crevasse out of which sound is born is the throat. The stream of heat carried the indeterminate vowel "e," turned to one side, coinciding with the consonantless alpha--so teach the linguists; and they teach that this tilted "e" or "a" into "ar," "al" turned into "ir," "ur." "U" is a semi-vowel. It is halfway between "u" and "w." In "u" we move our larynx: "uh-uh"--it was pronounced out of the throat. In expression of noise, heat (in the mouth cavity)--horrors. And behind the distinct sound slithered the snake of fever into the crevasses of the larynx. Allow the last sound to return unto itself, to the place where it leaves the throat, to the moments of its childhood, and it will see what crawled out, following it out of the hole, out of the depths.

Iaz, Az, Azia, Azy--flies into Europe with an ancient sound: iz Azii. In the Kaballa of Azia the ether of light is mentioned, unseen by the normal eye. Those dedicated to Azia see it. Perhaps it is seen in the dawn (na zare). Perhaps it is Nazarea--this Azia--

it is not on this earth. Where it is, there is
Paradise--All-Azia. It is Pant-Azia--it is
Fantazia. But Fantazia does exist there,
beyond the fiery cloud.

In the Hills

The hills are in their Sunday best,
I'm full of delight, I am young,
And inside these hills, I will rest,
And get a chill in my lungs.

Climbing up on a cliff
Comes a hunchback in grey,
With a pineapple gift
From an underground cave.

He's prancing in scarlet,
Glorifying the trees,
And the beard of this varlet
Makes many a breeze.

He sung
In low bass.
And he flung
A pineapple up into space.

And tracing an arc,
Lighting the sky very tall,
The pineapple fell in the dark
Into nothing at all.
This beautiful show
Made golden the dew
And they said down below,
"This is something new."

Down with a ringing
Came fires of gold,
To the cliffs they were bringing
The singing
Of dew when it's cold.

With a goblet of wine, just like
    a mouse
I crept up to the holm.
And the hunchback I doused,
With the silvery foam.

BLOK

I Sense Your Closeness

I sense your closeness. The years go by.
Only in my mind's eye, do I sense you.

The world's aflame, clear is the sky,
I wait alone, while loving true.

The world's aflame, the revelation's near,
But I'm afraid you'll change your face.

And a bold suspicion will appear,
Of what I know, there'll be no trace.

Oh how I'll tumble, bitterly and low,
Not conquering the dreams I think so true.

How clear the sky, I hope its radiance
    will show
But I'm afraid it won't be you.

BABEL

Cemetery At Kozin

A cemetery in a small Jewish place. Assyria and the mysterious decay of the East on the Volynian plains overgrown with tall grasses.

Carved grey stones with three—century—old letters. The crude stamped-out high reliefs, chopped on granite. Fish and lambs pictured over a dead man's head. Rabbis in fur hats. The rabbis' narrow loins are girded with straps. Under their eyeless faces, the wavy stone lines of curled beards. To the side, under a lightning-shattered oak, stands the vault of rabbi Azrael, killed by the cossacks of Bogdan Khmelnitsky. Four generations lie in this tomb, poor like a water-carrier's home; and the memorial stones, the mossy memorial stones, sing of them with a Bedouin's prayer:

"Azrael, son of Ananais, the mouth of Jehovah."
"Ilya, son of Azrael, a brain having undertaken hand-to-hand combat with oblivion."
"Wolff, son of Ilya, a prince kidnapped from the Torah in his nineteenth spring."
"Judah, son of Wolff, rabbi of Cracow and Prague."
"O death, O covetous one, a greedy thief, why did you not spare us, even once?"

MAYAKOVSKY

Brodvei (Broadway)

The asphalt is glass.
    I go and ring it.
The woods and the grass
    Are shaved.
To the north
    From the south
        We have "avenue"
To the west
    From the east
        We have "street-y"
And in the middle--
    What the builder did do!--
houses
    impossibly big.
Some houses
    their length to the stars.

Others--
    their length to the moon.
The Yankee
    is lazy
        to shlep on his soles:
Simple is his lift.
Local and
    Express elevators.
At 7
    the high tide of mankind,
At 17
    is the ebb.

The gears grind,
    ring and bam.

The people are dumb
    from the noise.

And maybe they slow
    down to chew <u>chevingam</u>
To throw out
    "Mek moni"

A mother
    has given
        her breast
            to her child.
The child
    With drops from his nose,
sucks away,
    as if it wasn't
        a breast, but a dollar.
He is occupied
    with "series bizness."

Work is over,
    Wrap your body
        in a completely
            electric wind.

If it's underground,
    take the <u>subvei</u>;
If to the sky,
    <u>elevaitor</u>.

The train-cars
    ride just under the smoke,
and rub the heels
    of houses.
and take their tails
    out
        on Brooklyn Bridge,
And hide
    in the burrows
        under the Hudson.

You're blind
    you're dazed.

But,
            like buckshot on a drum
From the fog
            to your noggin:
                "Kofe Maksvel
gud
            tu di lest drap."

Wait till you see
            how the lamps
                excavate the night,
well, I tell you,
            it's some little flame
You look to the left--
            "mother of mine!"
You look to the right--
            "oh, mother!"
There's a lot for the Moscow brothers to
            see.
Stay here more than a day.
It's New York.
            It's Brodvei.
Gau du yu-du!
I'm elated
            By New York City.
But
            My cap
                Will stay on my head.
The Soviets' pride
            Is special.
We look at the bourgeois
            From above.
6 August 1925
New York.

VOZNESENSKY

I'm Goya!

I'm Goya!
The enemy's pecked out the eyes from the
　　　craters, flying into the field
　　　furiously.

I'm Grief!
I'm the Groaning
Of war, of the hunger of cities in the
　　　snow of forty-one.

I'm Hunger!
I'm the Hoarse
Voice of the hung woman whose body, like a
　　　bell, swings bare on the square.

I'm Goya!
O Grapes
Of wrath! I've strewn a salvo to the west,
　　　of the ashes of the unbidden guest!
And pounded the stars into the memorial
　　　sky like nails.

I'm Goya.

Parabolic Ballad

Fate, like a rocket, flies a parabola
Often, in dusks, and rarer, in rainbows.

There was a fiery-red painter, Gaugin,
A Bohemian, formerly a trade agent.
To get to the Louvre from Montmartre
He
　　　made
　　　　　　a side trip to Java and Sumatra!

He overcame
       The weight of the earth.
Into their beer, the priests laughed with
       mirth
"The short way is closer, the parabola's
       strained
Isn't it better to copy what heaven's
       ordained?"
But he just took off, in a howling rocket
Through wind, knocking your ears and your
       block off.
Through the Louvre's main entrance, he
       never arrived.
But by a Parabola
       Angrily
              He came in through the side.

Close by on our block, there was a nice
       lass;
We studied together, we were in the same
       class.
Where didn't I go!
              And the devil took me away
To   the   Tbilissian   stars   of   Georgia,   far
away!

Forgive my foolish parabola
Chilly shoulders in black formal
Oh, how you glimmered in the dim Eternal.
Resilient and straight, like the whip on
       an antenna!
And yet I still fly
       Landing by them
By your earthy, chilly urgings
How hard is the parabola!

Sweeping away canons, prognoses, paragraphs,
Art arches on, love and history
On the parabolic trajectory.

To Siberia, it's leaving tonight.

But maybe, the straight way's more right?

EVTUSHENKO

The Beatnik Girl

The girl's from New York
But that isn't her place.
From neon lights
She's hidden her face.

Hateful's her world
There's no truth on her list.
It's all a big fake,
She'd rather go "twist."

Her hair is uncombed
Specs and sweater are beat,
This minus loves dancing
With thin heels on her feet.

Her world is a lie
From Writ to gazettes,
Montagues, Capuletes, yes,
Not Romeos, Juliets.

In deep thought are the trees,
The moon, too, looks like a beat
It staggers and falls
Down Milky Way Street.

Ever so careful, it's always alone
From bar to bar does it go.
And with beautiful cruelty
It lights up the city below.

All is cruel, the roofs and the
    trees
And above, not as mere fictions,
Are antennas for many t.v.'s,
Without Christ--crucifixions.

AKHMADULINA

The New Blast Furnace In the
Kemerovo Metallurgical Combine

Where the new blast furnace is growing,
There on high the work proceeds.
High stands a lad, the wind is blowing,
He's laughing, no danger he heeds.

Along the ledge he walks full of mirth,
At any time, yet, a misstep slight
Will send him hurling to the earth;
His head should get dizzy with fright.

Freely and sweetly he sighs;
He's been walking like this very far,
And sparks flare up from the pipes,
Like an August shooting star.

He's endlessly bold and has pleasure
To do this, but also he hopes
That the girl below will measure
The long meters that separate them both.

These girls, that is their fate,
To look, but rarely to care,
She likes something here, something
        great,
Greater than what keeps him up there.

But at the circus, every once in a
        night,
She gets anxious, in fear how she gawks.
For a gymnast, she pales out of fright
If on a tight rope he walks,

And, not betraying that he is phased
About girls forgetting his name,
Our lad independently gazes,
While the burners shoot forth their
    flame.

SELECTED BIBLIOGRAPHY

The following books are recommended for further reading.

Texts on History, Culture, Literature

Billington, James H. The Icon and the Axe: An Interpretive History of Russian Culture. New York: Random House, 1970.

Mirsky, Dmitry S. History of Russian Literature from its Beginnings to 1900. Edited by Francis J. Whitfield. New York: Random House, 1958.

Riasanovsky, Nicholas. A History of Russia. 3d ed. New York: Oxford University Press, 1977.

Smith, Hedrick. The Russians. New York: Quadrangle, 1976.

Treadgold, Donald W. Twentieth Century Russia. 5th ed. New York: Rand McNally, 1981.

Anthologies, Readers

Alexander, Alex E., ed. Russian Folklore: An Anthology in English Translation. Belmont, Mass.: Nordland, 1974.

Dmytryshyn, Basil, ed. Imperial Russia: A Source Book, 1700-1917. 2d ed. New York: Holt, Rinehart and Winston, 1974.

Dmytryshyn, Basil, ed. Medieval Russia: A Source Book, 900-1700. 2d ed. New York: Holt, Rinehart and Winston, 1973.

Guerney, Bernard, ed. Anthology of Russian Literature in the Soviet Period from Gorki to Pasternak. New York: Random House, 1960.

Guerney, Bernard, ed. Treasury of Russian Literature. New York: Vanguard, 1943.

Hamilian, Leo and Vera Wiren-Garczynski, ed. Seven Russian Short Novel Masterpieces. New York: Popular Library, 1967.

Obolensky, Dimitri, ed. Heritage of Russian Verse. Bloomington: Indiana University Press, 1976.

Segel, Harold, ed. Literature of Eighteenth-Century Russia: A History and Anthology. 2 v. New York: Dutton, 1967.

Zenkovsky, Serge A., ed. Medieval Russia's Epics, Chronicles and Tales. Rev. new ed. New York: Dutton, 1974.

Philosophy, Religion

Edie, James M., James P. Scanlan, and
Mary-Barbara Zeldin, ed. Russian
Philosophy. 3 v. Knoxville:
University of Tennessee Press, 1976.

Herzen, Alexander. My Past and Thoughts.
New York: Random House, 1974.

Ware, Timothy. The Orthodox Church.
Baltimore: Penguin, 1963.

Music, Art

Bowlt, John. Russian Art of the Avant
Garde. New York: Viking, 1976.

Dodge, Norton, ed. New Art from the
Soviet Union: The Known and the
Unknown. Washington: Acropolis,
1977.

Hamilton, George H. Art and Architecture
of Russia. 2d ed. Baltimore:
Pelican, 1976.

Leonard, Richard A. A History of Russian
Music. Reprint ed. Westport:
Greenwood, 1977.

Nineteenth-Century Russian Literature

Chernyshevsky, Nikolai G. What is to Be
Done? Edited by I. B. Turkevich.
New York: Random House, 1961.

Dostoevsky, Fyodor. The Adolescent.
Translated by Andrew MacAndrew.
Garden City, N.Y.: Doubleday, 1972.

Dostoevsky, Fyodor. Best Short Stories.
Translated by David Magarshack. New
York: Modern Library, 1964.

Dostoevsky, Fyodor. Brothers Karamazov.
Translated by Andrew MacAndrew. New
York: Bantam, 1970.

Dostoevsky, Fyodor. Crime and Punishment.
Translated by Constance Garnett. New
York: Modern Library, 1959.

Dostoevsky, Fyodor. The Devils. Translated by David Magarshack. Baltimore:
Penguin, 1954.

Dostoevsky, Fyodor. House of the Dead.
Translated by Constance Garnett. New
York: Dell, 1959.

Dostoevsky, Fyodor. The Idiot. Translated by Constance Garnett. New York:
Modern Library, 1935.

Dostoevsky, Fyodor. Notes from the Under-
ground, Poor People, Friend of the
Family. Translated by Constance
Garnett. New York: Dell, 1960.

Gogol, Nikolai. Dead Souls. Translated
by Andrew MacAndrew. New York:
Signet, 1961.

Gogol, Nikolai. Diary of a Madman and Other Stories. Translated by Andrew MacAndrew. New York: New American Library, 1961.

Gogol, Nikolai. Mirgorod: Four Tales. Translated by David Magarshack. New York: Crowell, 1969.

Gogol, Nikolai. Selected Passages from a Correspondence with Friends. Translated by Jesse Zeldin. Nashville: Vanderbilt University Press, 1969.

Goncharov, Ivan. A Common Story. Translated by Constance Garnett. Hyperion, Conn.: Hyperion Press, 1977.

Goncharov, Ivan. The Precipice. Translated by M. Bryant. Hyperion, Conn.: Hyperion Press, 1977.

Kuprin, Aleksandr. The Duel. Hyperion, Conn.: Hyperion Press, 1977.

Leskov, Nikolai. The Enchanted Pilgrim and Other Stories. Translated by David Magarshack. Hyperion, Conn.: Hyperion Press, 1977.

Leskov, Nikolai. Satirical Stories. Translated by William B. Edgerton. New York: Pegasus, 1969.

Reeve, Franklin D., ed. Nineteenth-Century Russian Plays. New York: Norton, 1973.

Saltykov-Shchedrin, Mikhail. The Golovlovs. Translated by Andrew MacAndrew. New York: Signet, 1961.

Tolstoy, Leo. Anna Karenina. Translated by David Magarshack. New York: Signet, 1961.

Tolstoy, Leo. Childhood, Boyhood, Youth. Translated by Rosemary Edmonds. Baltimore: Penguin, 1964.

Tolstoy, Leo. The Cossacks and the Raid. Translated by Andrew MacAndrew. New York: Signet, 1961.

Tolstoy, Leo. Death of Ivan Ilyich and Other Stories. Translated by Aylmer Maude. New York: Signet, 1960.

Tolstoy, Leo. Resurrection. Translated by Rosemary Edmonds. Baltimore: Penguin, 1966.

Tolstoy, Leo. Sebastopol. Ann Arbor: University of Michigan Press, 1961.

Tolstoy, Leo. War and Peace. Translated by Ann Dunnigan. New York: Signet, 1968.

Turgenev, Ivan. Fathers and Sons. Translated by George Reavey. New York: Signet, 1961.

Turgenev, Ivan. First Love and Other Stories. Translated by David Magarshack. New York: Norton, 1968.

Turgenev, Ivan. On the Eve. Translated
by Gilbert Gardiner. Baltimore:
Penguin, 1950.

Turgenev, Ivan. Rudin. Translated by
Richard Freeborn. Baltimore: Penguin,
1975.

Turgenev, Ivan. Sketches from a Hunter's
Album. Translated by Richard
Freeborn. Baltimore: Penguin, 1967.

Turgenev, Ivan. Virgin Soil. Translated
by Constance Garnett. New York: Grove
Press, 1977.

Twentieth-Century, Prerevolutionary Period, General Texts

Gibian, George and H. W. Tjalsma, ed.
Russian Modernism: Culture and the
Avant-Garde, 1900-1930. Ithaca:
Cornell University Press, 1976.

Slonim, Marc. From Chekhov to the
Revolution: Russian Literature, 1900-
1917. New York: Oxford University
Press, 1962.

Twentieth-Century, Prerevolutionary Literature

Bely, Andrey. St. Petersburg. Translated by John Cournos. New York:
Grove Press, 1959.

Bely, Andrey. Silver Dove. Translated
    by George Reavey. New York: Grove
    Press, 1974.

Blok, Aleksandr. Selected Poems. Edited
    by James Woodward. New York: Oxford
    University Press, 1968.

Bunin, Ivan. Dark Avenues and Other
    Stories. Translated by R. Hare.
    Hyperion, Conn.: Hyperion Press, 1977.

Chekhov, Anton. Eleven Stories. Trans-
    lated by Ronald Hingley. New York:
    Oxford University Press, 1976.

Chekhov, Anton. Anton Chekhov: Four
    Plays. Translated by David
    Magarshack. New York: Hill and Wang,
    1969.

Chekhov, Anton. Chekhov: Selected
    Stories. New York: Signet, 1960.

Gorky, Maxim. My Childhood. Translated
    by Ronald Wilks. Baltimore: Penguin,
    1966.

Reeve, Franklin D., ed. Twentieth-Century
    Russian Plays: An Anthology. New
    York: Norton, 1973.

Sologub, Fyodor. Petty Demon. Trans-
    lated by Andrew Field. Bloomington:
    Indiana University Press, 1970.

Soviet Literature, General Texts

Brown, Edward J. Russian Literature
    Since the Revolution. Chicago:
    Collier Books, 1969.

Dunham, Vera S. In Stalin's Time:
    Stalinist Fiction and Soviet Society.
    New York: Cambridge University Press,
    1976.

Soviet Literature

Babel, Isaac. Collected Stories. Trans-
    lated by Walter Morison. New York:
    New American Library, 1955.

Evtushenko, Evgeny. Yevtushenko's
    Reader: The Spirit of Elbe, A
    Precocious Biography, Poems. New
    York: Dutton, 1966.

Mayakovsky, Vladimir. The Bedbug and
    Selected Poetry. Edited by Patricia
    Blake, Max Hayward and George Reavey.
    Bloomington: Indiana University Press,
    1975.

Olesha, Yury. Envy and Other Works.
    Translated by Andrew MacAndrew.
    Garden City: Doubleday, 1967.

Pasternak, Boris. Doctor Zhivago. Trans-
    lated by Max Hayward. New York:
    Signet, 1958.

Pilnyak, Boris. The Naked Year. Trans-
    lated by Alexander Tulloch. Ann
    Arbor: Ardis, 1975.

Reavey, George, ed. The New Russian
    Poets. New York: October Press, 1966.

Reeve, Franklin D., ed. Great Soviet
    Short Stories. New York: Dell, 1962.

Sholokhov, Mikhail. And Quiet Flows the
    Don. Translated by H. C. Stevens. New
    York: Random House, 1965.

Sholokhov, Mikhail. The Don Flows Home to
    the Sea. Translated by H. C. Stevens.
    New York: Random House, 1965.

Solzhenitsyn, Alexander. August 1914.
    Translated by Michael Glenny. New
    New York: Farrar, Straus and Giroux,
    1972.

Solzhenitsyn, Alexander. Cancer Ward.
    Translated by Rebecca Frank. New
    New York: Dial, 1974.

Solzhenitsyn, Alexander. The First
    Circle. Translated by Thomas
    Whitney. New York: Bantam, 1969.

Solzhenitsyn, Alexander. The Gulag
    Archipelago. Translated by Thomas
    Whitney. New York: Harper-Row, 1974.

Solzhenitsyn, Alexander. The Gulag
    Archipelago: Two. Translated by
    Thomas Whitney. New York: Harper-
    Row, 1975.

Solzhenitsyn, Alexander. The Gulag
    Archipelago: Three. Translated by
    Harry Willets. New York: Harper-
    Row, 1977.

Solzhenitsyn, Alexander. <u>One Day in the Life of Ivan Denisovich</u>. Translated by Ralph Parker. New York: Dutton, 1963.

~vgeny. <u>We.</u> Translated by New York: Dutton,

<u>Nervous People and</u> ranslated by Hugh ι Gordon. Bloomington: Press, 1975.